PASSAGE TO PASCH

Michael Drumm

Passage to Pasch

Revisiting the Catholic Sacraments

the columba press

First published in 1998 by

the columba press

55A Spruce Avenue, Stillorgan Industrial Park
Blackrock, Co Dublin

Cover by Bill Bolger
Cover photographs by permission of Bord Fáilte
Origination by The Columba Press
Printed in Ireland by Genprint Ltd, Dublin
ISBN 1 85607 176 6

Contents

To my mother and father

Introduction

The first course that I was asked to teach in theology at third level was on the sacraments. I thought that I had drawn the short straw. My own theological formation would have suggested that christology or revelation or God were more interesting areas of study as sacramental theology did not appear to have been renewed in the same way as other disciplines. It still seemed to be dominated by issues of rubric and law to the near exclusion of a more dynamic personal and biblical theology. But I was wrong.

In my efforts to speak meaningfully about the sacraments over the last several years, I have discovered that there is no more important pastoral issue facing the Catholic Church in Ireland and internationally than the renewal of its ritual life. Ireland and its history is a particularly interesting context in which to study the nature of religious ritual given the lively interaction of Christianity and traditional religion over almost two millennia. The riches and treasures of this Irish tradition should not be underestimated.

One of the main themes of this book is the contrast of the iconophile and the iconoclast, the contrast of the one who loves image, symbol and ritual with the one who breaks and destroys these in bouts of theological purity. There are many lessons to be learned about the dangers of such puritanism. Hopefully we can construct a future that does not repeat all the mistakes of the past.

I acknowledge my debt to several educational institutions who, in giving me the opportunity to teach, opened up endless new horizons for research and reflection; in particular Mater Dei Institute of Education, Dublin; also St Angela's College of Education, Sligo and the Marianella Centre for Renewal, Dublin.

I thank my colleagues and friends whose encouragement taught me the value and significance of theology for our times. Thanks to all of those who read parts of the manuscript, especially Liam Bergin who read it all and whose comments helped me enormously; to Dermot Lane for his kindness and interest in my theological studies; to Tom Gunning and Aileen Young for composing a very suitable title. But most of all I express my gratitude to the countless students and parishioners whose questions and reflections have taught me far more than I could ever have hoped to learn.

Michael Drumm
6 January 1998
Feast of the Epiphany of Our Lord

Prologue

For this is what I received from the Lord, and in turn passed on to you: that on the same night that he was betrayed, the Lord Jesus took some bread, and thanked God for it and broke it, and he said, 'This is my body, which is for you; do this as a memorial of me'. In the same way he took the cup after supper, and said, 'This cup is the new covenant in my blood. Whenever you drink it, do this as a memorial of me'. Until the Lord comes, therefore, every time you eat this bread and drink this cup, you are proclaiming his death.

St Paul, 1 Corinthians 11:23-26

A story with two endings

David lived in Corinth. He was a member of the thriving local Jewish community. He attended the synagogue every sabbath, studied the Torah diligently and was careful about the traditional dietary laws. In truth he was proud of his identity. But he was also well integrated in the secular life of the city of Corinth where he had an excellent job working as a sculptor carving Corinthian capitals. Nothing excited him more than to sit on the high hill above the city looking down on the great ships; his heart throbbed with excitement as he dreamt of their destinations — Egypt and Israel. Neither he nor any member of his family for several generations had ever been to either of these lands which were so much a part of who he was. But the day would come, yes, the day would come.

Looking eastwards out over the Aegean Sea, David would say to himself: 'for the peace of Jerusalem pray, peace be to your homes, may peace reign in your walls, in your palaces peace; blessed be Yahweh!'

The day did come. It was 53 AD, according to the Christian calendar, when David finally got the chance to visit Israel, the city of Jerusalem and the temple. He was quite simply overwhelmed by joy. He arrived in the city late one evening and got lodgings in one of the many hostels that thrived in the vicinity of the Damascus Gate. He didn't sleep that night and rose as early as the cock crew. He opened the shutters on his window to the most wonderful sight he ever saw – the rising sun shining on the parapet of the temple. David was overcome with tears of joy as the words of the songs and prayers that he had learned as a child flooded his mind: 'by the rivers of Babylon we sat and wept remembering Zion'; 'I rejoiced when I heard them say, let us go to God's house and now our feet are standing within your gates, O Jerusalem'.

Breakfast was a quick affair as David was in a hurry; he only had three days in Jerusalem and he was going to make the most of them. Walking through the narrow streets, bursting with traders, David couldn't keep himself from looking upwards, for every time he turned a corner he got a different glimpse of the porticoes of the temple. And then finally he exited a narrow street and there it stood before him in all its glory – the temple. He fell to his knees and said aloud: 'I thank you Lord with all my heart, you have heard the words of my mouth. In the presence of the angels I will bless you. I will adore before your holy temple.'

In the precincts of the temple he started talking to two other young men who happened to be from Galilee. They had greeted him in Aramaic but he couldn't respond so they used their broken Greek. It was great to meet up with them and they brought him through the various courts and helped him to make a deposit for the sacrifice of a lamb at Passover. David did all the things that a true pilgrim would do: he walked around the temple, he prayed, he lit candles in memory of his ancestors, he bought mementoes and trinkets for his younger brothers and sisters. Yes, this had been the greatest day of his life!

On the way down from the temple, one of his two new-found friends from Galilee, Philip was his name, the other was called Jude, asked him had he ever heard of Jesus of Nazareth. David had to confess that he didn't even know where Nazareth was, never mind knowing any of its occupants. They told him a remarkable story about this Jesus who had preached the dawning of God's kingdom but who had been put to death by the religious and political leaders. And then came the really interesting bit – God had raised him from the dead and they believed that he was the Messiah, the Christ of God. David asked could he meet this extraordinary figure but that proved to be a bit of a problem given that this Jesus now shared God's own life. However, in a vain attempt to convince David, they brought him to see the empty tomb. He raised the usual objections that the body could have been stolen or removed and hidden. They spoke to him about the eye-witnesses of the risen Jesus but it transpired that most of them were dead or had scattered far and wide. And had any of these followers been raised from the dead? No, not yet! David was coming quickly to the conclusion that these Galileans were visionaries in the worst sense of the word. His mother had told him to be careful in Jerusalem because he'd meet all sorts of strange people. She was right. No, this Jesus wasn't alive; death had taken him just like everyone else before him. On the ship returning to Corinth, David pondered on all that had happened in Jerusalem. He recalled that he had indeed heard this name 'Christian' before; his father had warned him about this new group which had caused some difficulties in

the synagogue in Corinth. Little did his father know how right
he was. 'Just think how gullible those two poor fools were,' he
thought to himself, 'but then, what would you expect of
Galileans?' David remained one of the most faithful and active
members of the thriving Jewish community in Corinth.

A second ending

On the way down from the temple, one of his two new-
found friends from Galilee, Philip was his name, the other
was called Jude, asked him had he ever heard of Jesus of
Nazareth. David had to confess that he didn't even know
where Nazareth was, never mind knowing any of its occupants. They told him a remarkable story about this Jesus who
had preached the dawning of God's kingdom but who had
been put to death by the religious and political leaders. And
then came the really interesting bit – God had raised him
from the dead and they believed that he was the Messiah, the
Christ of God. David asked could he meet this extraordinary
figure but that proved to be a bit of a problem given that this
Jesus now shared God's own life. However, they invited him
to come to a house on a narrow back street that evening where
what they called the brethren would meet for the breaking of
bread. Given that he had little else to do after sunset, he agreed
to go along. About thirty people, women and men, young
and old, showed up and they made him feel very welcome.
They sang psalms and blessed the Lord Yahweh in much the
same way as David did at home. But then they started telling
stories about this man Jesus. One woman sitting next to
David told a really interesting story about Jesus meeting a
Samaritan woman at a well; she said that she had heard it
from her mother. After some time, they baptised two young
men and David asked to be baptised as well. Then they laid
hands upon the newly baptised and called what they termed
the Holy Spirit upon them. Finally there was the breaking of

bread in the midst of which they spoke of Jesus' self-sacrific-
ing death and the last supper. His mother had told him to be
careful in Jerusalem because he'd meet all sorts of strange people. She couldn't have expected that he would meet up with
such a dynamic community. There had been a real sense that
though this Jesus had died, he was indeed alive and present.
On the ship returning to Corinth, David pondered on all that
had happened in Jerusalem. He recalled that he had indeed
heard this name 'Christian' before; his father had warned him
about this new group which had caused some difficulties in
the synagogue in Corinth. Little did his father know what was
going to happen in Jerusalem. 'I must find out more about
this community in Corinth,' he thought to himself, 'and I
mustn't forget to write letters to my friends in Galilee.' David
became one of the most faithful and active members of the
newly-emerging Christian community in Corinth.

* * *

The origins of Christian faith do not lie in empty tombs or
strange visions but in the fellowship of those who believed
that Jesus was alive. In all of the gospel accounts of visions of
the risen Jesus the disciples fail to recognise him, but they do
recognise him in the breaking of bread, the waters of baptism,
the laying on of hands and the forgiveness of sin. For decades
the followers of the Way, soon to be called Christians, gathered for these communal rituals through which their identity
was established and nourished. Later on they wrote down
what had survived through ritual and memory. This is why it
is untrue to say that Christians are people of the book; instead
the book is the book of the people. The people and their rituals
existed long before the written scriptures. That is why it is so
important for Christians to have a real feel for the nature and
meaning of ritual.

The Nature of Ritual

'Yahweh brought us here and gave us this land, a land where milk and honey flow. Here then I bring the first fruits of the produce of the soil that you, Yahweh, have given me.' You must then lay them before Yahweh your God, and bow down in the sight of Yahweh your God. Then you are to feast on all the good things Yahweh has given you, you and your household, and with you the Levite and the stranger who lives among you.

Deuteronomy 26:9-11

Every society that has ever existed attempted to create cosmos out of chaos. In the cold harsh physical reality of our planet societies, cultures and civilisations have used myth, symbol and ritual to construct an amazing world of meaning in the face of the obvious meaninglessness of human existence. For what are the reasons for hope between womb and tomb? These passages of human birth and death are statistically very common; another human is born, another one dies – it matters little at a societal level. But in the life of the individual and the lives of significant others these passages are all important; one could go so far as to say that little else matters at all. Yet the key questions remain. Why was I born? Where did I come from? Why am I conscious of my own consciousness? Why will I die? What happens through death? Questions concerning origins, destiny and consciousness have in one sense plagued the human spirit, in another sense they have enabled us as a species to attain our greatest achievements in artistic, religious and cultural expression. Faced with the deep-rooted insecurity at the heart of existence, humans have turned to the same rituals and symbols to interpret their experiences. The early Christians took existing rituals and symbols and, casting them in the new story of the death and resurrection of Jesus of Nazareth, made the most amazing claims about the dignity and destiny of human life. To truly understand the evolution of sacramental expression in the Catholic Church one must first explore the pervasiveness of mythic, symbolic and ritual expression in the social experience of the human family.

What makes this area of study so exciting is that it is an important dimension of the modern discovery of historical consciousness. One of the key features of the modern enlightenment is the awakening of a sense of history, a keen awareness that things have not always been the way they are now, that social, religious and political institutions and ideas have gone through an overwhelming process of change since the dawn of history. Bernard Lonergan characterised this revolution in modern thought as a shift from a classical conception of culture to an empirical understanding of culture;[1] a shift from the certainties of a normative culture in terms of tastes, languages, beliefs and mores (a cultured person would have certain tastes, speak certain languages, hold certain beliefs and follow certain mores), to an awareness that there are as many different cultures as there have been efforts to humanise the world, that there is no normative culture but rather endless interactions of humans with the environments in which they find themselves. This interaction has given rise to language and literature, science and mathematics, education and

1. See his article 'The Transition from a Classicist World-view to Historical-mindedness' in W.F.J. Ryan and B.J. Tyrrel eds., *A Second Collection: Papers by Bernard J.F. Lonergan S.J.*, London: Darton, Longman and Todd 1974, pp. 1-9.

medicine, the state and the city, artistic expression and philosophical reflection. But we have only become aware of this complexity over the last two centuries, even though *Homo sapiens* has been thinking about things for close on two hundred thousand years. All of this is the wonderful creation of the human spirit. With this awareness of what humanity has achieved, new sciences emerged to interpret the vast field of historical data: archaeology, philology, ethnography, anthropology and sociology. These new sciences seek to interpret how earlier and existing cultures and civilisations understand and express themselves. In other words, when we look back at a long since extinct civilisation we are trying to understand how that civilisation understood itself and how it expressed that self-understanding. As the various human sciences attempted to interpret the historical and contemporary expressions of human self-understanding, it became clear that personal and social meaning is mediated through symbol and ritual. Lonergan comments:

> Traditionally man was defined with abstract generality as .... the rational animal. More concretely today he is regarded as the symbolic animal, whose knowledge is mediated by symbols, whose actions are informed by symbols, whose existence in its most characteristic features is constituted by a self-understanding and by commitments specified by symbols. On the abstract view, man was understood as nature. On the relatively recent view, man is understood as historic, for the symbols that inform his being vary with the cultures into which he is born, and the cultures themselves change with the passage of time. They emerge, they develop, they flourish, they influence one another, they can go astray, vanish with their former carriers, only to reappear with fresh vitality and vigor grafted upon new hosts.[2]

2. Frederick E. Crowe, *A Third Collection: Papers by Bernard J.F. Lonergan S.J.*, London: Geoffrey Chapman 1985, p. 115.

In other words, we have moved away from an over emphasis
on rationality in our self-understanding and we've begun to
revisit the ancient wellsprings of symbol and ritual. In these
wells there is an extraordinary richness, as symbol and ritual
are the carriers, the mediators, of millennia of accumulated
wisdom. But it is all too easy to miss out on their significance.
Some reflection is required in order to treasure the power of
symbol and ritual. Symbols should be contrasted with simple
signs. A sign, think of a road sign or traffic signals, is simple.
It is part of a closed system with one clear reference; if you do
not know what it means then it is easy to find out. Symbols
on the contrary are complex; they are part of an open system
where new meanings can be added and there are a multiplicity
of possible references. Think of a smile, a tear, a human
corpse. These can symbolise radically different things to different people. They evoke varied responses. Even though they
exist in and of their own right, they can connote something
other, deeper, unspoken, unspeakable. Symbols elicit endless
interpretations and re-interpretations and, unquestionably,
misinterpretations. Of course, you can inhabit a reductionist
world where only the biological or physiological construction
of any object is of interest; but just imagine how much your
world would literally be reduced if tears were interpreted as
nothing more than a body fluid, smiles were interpreted only
as changes in facial musculature and corpses were purely ob-
jects that needed to be quickly disposed of in case of disease.
All of these interpretations, whilst true, are terribly limited.
There is far greater depth in life than meets the eye and the
only access to this non-visible world is through a sensitivity to
symbol. Such sensitivity opens the prospect of entering
worlds and dimensions that the reductionist mindset doesn't
even know exists. The invitation is there to everyone to visit
these wonderful worlds, to perceive new and unimagined dimensions, to open the locks on the boring two dimensional

world that we so often inhabit. And the good news, so seldom announced, is that this invitation is free; everyone, old and young, rich and poor, male and female, can undertake this journey of the imagination which is the longest journey of all because it is the journey inwards to the depths of one's own life. On this journey of symbolic self-discovery, some of the great moments are ritualised, for it is in good ritual that our symbolic sense is heightened and dormant symbols have the power to speak anew.

It is only over the last one hundred years that we have become aware of the centrality of ritual in our lives. Modern men and women born of the enlightenment had dismissed rituals as pertaining only to a primitive state of consciousness, apt behaviour for a child or an ignorant tribe but something that the modern mind had long since left behind. Indeed the enlightenment could almost be defined as the process of freeing people from the religious and civil rituals that had kept them in bondage for centuries. The rise of modern science, industry and the city, what's commonly referred to as modernity, was meant to have heralded the demise of all primitive rituals. No longer would people demean their fully grown humanity by participation in age old rites but since people had come of age they would free themselves from the superstitious powers that had long held them captive. Religious rituals would die in much the same way as the certainties of childhood give way to the searing critique of adolescence. And it did happen. In the post-industrial revolution urban world, religion entered a period of apparently terminal decline; religious ritual became the preserve of people who were often old, sometimes odd, overwhelmingly rural, predominantly female. Given time it would surely fade away. But the extraordinary fact is that it hasn't. Indeed religious rituals, in the broadest sense, are undergoing a remarkable renaissance. Since the 1960s there has been a growing reaction against materialism, rationalism and technological pragmatism as people seek new paths to explore the spiritual, the ethical and the endless horizons of the inner life. Whether all of these pathways are compatible with being a Christian is a question we will return to later; for now the crucial question concerns the role of ritual in human societies.

From rites of passage to ritual in society today

It was only in this century, with the development of new sciences such as ethnography and cultural anthropology, that an appreciation of the function and meaning of ritual developed. The key figure was Arnold van Gennep who published the ground breaking *Rites de Passage* in 1909.[3] Here for the first time rites of passage were identified and analysed. Van Gennep isolated rites associated with key passages or transitions in life – pregnancy, birth, adolescence, betrothal, marriage, death. In pre-modern cultures (i.e. the tribe or the village) he argued that 'beneath a multiplicity of forms, either consciously expressed or merely implied, a typical pattern always recurs: *the pattern of the rites of passage.*'[4] Within these rites of passage he noted rites of separation, rites of transition and rites of incorporation. In other words, the subject of the ritual is in some way ritually separated from his peers, undergoes rites which bring about a major transition in his life and then, through rites of incorporation, re-enters his society with a new social status. Take, for example, the adolescent male passing from the asexual world of childhood to the sexual world of adulthood, passing from the innocence of childhood to the responsibility of adulthood; in many pre-modern contexts the adolescent was taken by adult males to a secret place for a definite period of time where he underwent various rites

3. Arnold van Gennep, *Rites of Passage*, translated by Monika B. Vizedom and Gabrielle L. Caffee, London: Routledge and Kegan Paul 1960.
4. Van Gennep, p. 191.

of transition, often involving hardship and struggle; on com-
pletion of these rites he returned to the tribe or village where
he was incorporated anew as an adult male. In other words,
the adolescent had died to childhood and had been ritually
reborn to adulthood. In the course of a short period of time
he had crossed the threshold from childhood to adulthood.
This idea of transitions associated with key threshold moments in life, and characterised by death to one social status
or cosmic context and rebirth to another, forms the core of
van Gennep's insight. He said that

> there are always new thresholds to cross: the thresholds of
> summer and winter, of a season or a year, of a month or a
> night; the thresholds of birth, adolescence, maturity and
> old age; the threshold of death and that of the afterlife –
> for those who believe in it.[5]

Around these threshold experiences human cultures have
evolved rites of separation whereby we let go of the old, rites
of transition whereby we are changed, and rites of incorporation whereby we are reborn to the new. To all of these he gave
the umbrella title – rites of passage.

When one attempts to analyse the role of ritual behaviour
in human communities, the theologian has much to learn
from cultural anthropologists, sociologists and ethnogra-
phers. The work of Arnold van Gennep is particularly instructive but that of Victor Turner is probably even more important.[6] Turner accepted van Gennep's basic outline of the

---

5. Van Gennep, pp. 189-90.

6. The most important of Turner's works are: *The Forest of Symbols*, New York:
Cornell University Press 1967; *The Ritual Process: Structure and Anti-Structure*,
New York: Cornell University Press 1969; *Dramas, Fields and Metaphors: Symbolic
Action in Human Society*, New York: Cornell University Press 1974, and with
Edith Turner, *Image and Pilgrimage in Christian Culture*, New York: Columbia
University Press 1978. Many other authors have drawn on the work of Turner
and van Gennep in developing the area of study known as ritual studies. Amongst
the more important works are: Catherine Bell, *Ritual Theory, Ritual Practice*,

structure of rites of passage but he believed that one could
identify aspects of these rites in rituals that were not associated
with the major passages in life. He adapted van Gennep's
model in his analysis of the three-fold character of ritual as
separation, liminality and reaggregation.[7] The participants in
the ritual separate themselves from the ordinary in some way
– through dress, behaviour, gathering, journeying, posture,
etc. They do so in order to experience the liminal, to experience *communitas*. What is this liminal/*communitas* experience? There is a sense of comradeship and communion which
normal social structures often inhibit, a loss of self and ego-
boundaries, a powerful sense of at-oneness, an awakening of
the transcendent dimension through myth and symbol. It is
an encounter with life on the threshold (hence the term liminal
from the latin *limen*, "threshold"), the periphery, the margins
(up the mountain, away at the shrine, on the island, at the
ruin) with a new sense of power based on nature and the sacred. The experience of liminality is anti-structural; the structures and hierarchies of society are abrogated through varied
phenomena such as fasting, silence, going bare-foot, wearing
masks, dancing, and these processes produce a sense of *communitas* premised on the qualities of lowliness, sacredness and
comradeship. This liminal/*communitas* experience is liberating, immediate and concrete; one encounters others and what
is usually called 'reality' in a new and unmediated way which
can often give the participant a radically different perspective

Oxford: Oxford University Press 1992; Robert L. Cohn, *The Shape of Sacred
Space: Four Biblical Studies*, AAR Studies in Religion, No. 23, Chico, California:
Scholars Press 1981; Mary Douglas, *Purity and Danger: An Analysis of the Concepts
of Pollution and Taboo*, London: Routledge and Kegan Paul 1966; Tom F. Driver,
*The Magic of Ritual: Our Need for Liberating Rites that Transform Our Lives and
Our Communities*, San Francisco: Harper 1991; James Shaughnessy ed., *The Roots
of Ritual*, Grand Rapids: Eerdmans 1973; Jonathan Z. Smith, *To Take Place:
Toward Theory in Ritual*, Chicago: University of Chicago Press 1987.
7. See V. Turner, *The Ritual Process: Structure and Anti-Structure*, pp. 94-203.

on life. And then the participants reaggregate, they return to the structures of *societas* where all know their place. But their identity has been renewed and the memory of *communitas* can become a subversive presence.

True, effective ritual is characterised then by these three aspects: separation, liminality and reaggregation. Let's look at these three dimensions again to ensure that their meaning is clear. To enter the ritual ambience is in some sense to separate oneself from the ordinary. People often do this by returning to a special place, entering a church or a holy place, going on retreat or pilgrimage, adapting the familiar place in terms of light or odour or sound or posture. They do all this with a purpose — that of experiencing the liminal: that space in human life where awe and mystery are encountered, where differences are transcended, where there is evocation of what is unseen and linguistically inexpressible, where identity is renewed. The very separation from the ordinary facilitates encounter with the liminal. Going on pilgrimage, being silent on retreat, participating in the dance, working with clay, leads to forgetfulness of self and discovery of a new dimension of who we are. The strange rituals of fasting, silence, dancing, abrogate social differences and facilitate a sense of wonder and awe. Having experienced the liminal, the participants reaggregate; they return to the ordinary refreshed, nourished, empowered with a renewed sense of identity. The community of the liminal experience is replaced by society and its structures where each one knows their place, where life is structured according to definite expectations.

That is ritual at its best. But rituals atrophy and decay, descending into the realms of empty ritualism with its pseudo-liminality. Participants still go through the motions but there is no sense of *communitas,* no renewal of identity. People still go to the church, the shrine, the holy place but this ritualistic behaviour has become so much a part of the structure of life that there is no separation, no liminality and no need for reaggregation since there was no separation in the first place. As the people of the tribe, the village and the agrarian world literally move into the modern world – the world of industry, mass education and the city – their traditional rituals are opened to question and often to ridicule. Slowly but surely many people begin to drift away from the rituals that were obligatory in the village, the tribe or the early agrarian society. These obligatory rituals were classically rites of passage associated with cosmic or biological passages; you could not be a part of the particular society without participating in these rituals for it was exactly through them that one was incorporated into the society. Throughout the world people leave their tribal, village or agrarian context (let's call them 'primitive societies' for short, while remembering that the word 'primitive' should not be interpreted pejoratively) for varied reasons; most are forced to move by the power of economic market forces while some want to leave in order to escape the deadening ritualism of primitive societies as the rituals atrophy and decay. Those who were forced to leave as economic migrants at first cling on to their rituals but, through a process of ridicule, social conformism and the need for an economically more efficient lifestyle, they slowly abandon these earlier rites until they become just a part of folk memory. Yet for both of these groups, the economic migrants and those who wanted to escape, the need for ritual does not disappear but is expressed in a new way.

Ritual expression in the modern world is different from that in the primitive society in one key respect: primitive rituals are characterised by obligation, modern rituals by choice. Furthermore, ritual behaviour tends to migrate into the private world of individuals where it is linked with leisure time activities which do not detract from one's economic efficiency. In the traditional rituals of the primitive society the key function of the rites of passage was the communication of the *sacra;* one encountered the sacred depths of existence before being reborn anew. As these rites decay nothing sacred is communicated and so modern people freely choose other ways to encounter the *sacra;* they do so through music and drama, theatre and film, literature and sport, and increasingly through consciousness-raising techniques and depth psychology.[8] These then become the rituals of modernity; notice some of their key characteristics – participation is voluntary and during one's free time, there is no major process of separation or reaggregation as in primitive rituals, and the experience is normally private as the participants retreat very quickly to their homes or apartments without any great sense of *communitas* having been created. These contrasts with primitive rituals are important but the ultimate contrast is this: modern people can wear the masks, prepare the special foods, engage in the dance, paint their faces, tell the stories, go to the hallowed place and so on, but they do so with a different consciousness for we can never encounter the earth or the other world or the dead or the gods or our ancestors in the way that the participants in primitive rituals did. Although ritual remains important, it inevitably changes in the modern world. Some even go so far as to claim that the only way we as modern people can retrieve the rituals of primitive societies is through drama and music; that we erect a sacred space in our secular world called a theatre and only within it can we revisit the sacred spaces of earlier generations. In Brian Friel's *Dancing at Lughnasa* the *communitas* experienced on occasion amongst the family in Ballybeg is replaced by the bleak anonymity of the urban dias-

8. In Turner's terminology these are liminoid genres of phenomena. He uses the term 'liminoid' to describe ritual behaviour which is freely chosen as distinct from the obligatory nature of most rituals in primitive societies. See V. Turner, *Image and Pilgrimage in Christian Culture*, pp. 231-32 and 253.

pora where two of the sisters disappear and die destitute.[9] All
of us must journey from Ballybeg to the city but the great
danger is that we lose our identity in the process. No simple
solution to this modern problem is available. Music and
dance are potent forces for kindling the imagination but religious ritual also offers the possibility of celebrating memory
in a way that enriches the soul and nourishes identity. On the
journey from Ballybeg to the city only memory and hope can
save us. Religious rituals, with their sensitivity to the sacred
and the archaic, might awaken a sense of who we are. If these
rituals fail us, then we are likely to be lost in the anonymity of
forgetfulness and despair.

There is one last aspect of ritual expression in the modern
world that is important to note. *Communitas* and the structured society are always in tension; the former is anti-structure
while the latter is constituted by hierarchies, organisations
and institutions. As long as a ritual provides a *communitas/*
liminal experience then the ritual will be anti-structure; but
when a ritual descends into the realms of pseudo-liminality
then it becomes nothing more than an expression of the existing structure. This is what tends to happen when rituals become institutionalised; some will simply fade away and die,
others will be renewed not least by those who live on the margins. Only a small number of people can live in a *communitas,*
anti-structural environment all the time, whilst most of us
live in very definite structures. These people like living on the
edge without order or structure and can happily accept chaos,
insecurity, poverty and lack of social identity. You find them
indulging in the craziest of adventures – climbing mountains
best left alone, crossing seas in vessels more suited to ponds,
hitching around the world instead of armchair travelling, re-
nouncing a comfortable lifestyle to live amongst the poorest

9. Brian Friel, *Dancing at Lughnasa*, London: Faber and Faber 1990. The play was
first performed at the Abbey Theatre, Dublin, on 24 April 1990.

of the poor. This sense of life on the edge, the periphery, the margins, is the real key to *communitas*/liminal experience since we all desire to know something of the grandeur of the mountain top, the awesomeness of the ocean, the detachment of the hitcher, the freedom of the one who chooses poverty over comfort and it is only when a ritual gives people such an experience that it can be described as anti-structural. Given that we now live in an incredibly structured environment – think of the corporate business world with its deadening routines of dress, behaviour, expectations and language – it is not surprising that, as before, creativity emerges from the margins. Artists, writers, philosophers, mystics go to the edge, the margins of their experience, and it is from these liminal spaces that *communitas* resurges to offer alternatives to the dominant structures. This is an important key to the renewal of rituals.

Rites of fertility and rites of initiation

All of the issues that we have addressed so far apply to rituals as they evolve over centuries. But while there was no distinction between religious and secular rituals in primitive societies, there are particular issues raised in the history of religions that are especially significant for understanding the nature of ritual. These issues revolve around the distinction between rites of fertility and rites of initiation, between what one might call an iconophile approach and an iconoclastic approach.

Iconophilia is the love of icons, images, symbols and rituals; iconophiles allow the imagination to express their religious beliefs, hopes and fears; the great theological temptation of the iconophile is idolatry, the temptation to equate the divine with the icon or the image or the symbol or the ritual.

Iconoclasm is the hatred of the latter precisely because the symbol or ritual can become identified with the divine; iconoclasts are image breakers because of the fear of idolatry; the theological temptation of iconoclasm is to deny the imagination any religious freedom in its solemn embrace of the sacred scriptures; for the iconoclast the word must be trusted while the image must be broken.

At the very origins of primitive religious consciousness were rituals associated with the fertility of the land occurring at key climatic and agricultural moments of the calendar. These rites were intended to insure against hunger through honouring the productive gods of the land. All religions trace their origins to land-based ritual. This is true even of those which are most iconoclastic concerning their pagan forebears. Take Judaism, which with its first two commandments is probably the most iconoclastic of all religions. Its three great temple feasts – Passover, Pentecost and Tabernacles – all had an agricultural origin. Passover emerged from the two feasts of Mazzoth (or unleavened bread), which was linked to the start of the barley harvest, and the festival of the slaughter of the yearling lamb for protection during the crucial period of spring lambing. Since the start of the harvest and lambing seasons coincide in Palestine the two feasts became the one great Jewish celebration of Passover. Prior to this they constituted festivals of the first fruits of the harvest. Pentecost or the Feast of Weeks took place fifty days later (7x7+1) at the end of the wheat harvest; so the original bounty of Pentecost is not the Spirit but the harvest. There is a lot of debate over the meaning of Tabernacles or Booths but there is no doubt about its agricultural overtones. The people lived in temporary tents or booths for the fruit (especially grape) harvest, followed by a week of great merriment since the ingathering of the harvest was complete.

As these old festivals and rituals are subsumed in a new 'religious' context, something very interesting occurs. Theology becomes iconophile regarding the new meanings and radically iconoclastic with respect to the earlier 'pagan' connotations. Take, for example, the Jewish feast of Passover. In the embrace of the new story of the exodus from Egypt (iconophilia), Jewish theology vehemently rejected the older traditions associated with the harvest and lambing (iconoclasm). This struggle between iconophilia and iconoclasm echoes throughout history. In some cases new religious movements literally broke, burned and tried to bury every vestige of earlier beliefs. The remains of such breaking, burning and burying are strewn across our planet, evidence of a deep theological distrust of the imagination. Such distrust has meant that individuals, communities and sometimes complete civilisations were broken, burned and buried in the name of religious orthodoxy. The iconoclastic fundamentalism of later religious adherents is one of the most commonly defining and objectionable aspects of mainstream religions. This is amongst the most important of all questions in theology, for simple iconoclasm is a cop out and turns theology into an ideologically objectionable discipline. Yet such iconoclasm has been the norm. A few outstanding examples will suffice to make this point.

The fourth century was a defining period in Christian history. In the first years of the century Christians suffered one of their most terrible persecutions at the hands of the emperor Diocletian. But the end of this same century saw power exercised by Christians for the first time in their history and the results for pagan traditions were catastrophic, not least in the loss of the wonderful library of Alexandria. Theodosius the Great, one of the most ardent iconoclasts of all time, outlawed all non-Christian images and rituals in 392. In the process, the altar of Zeus in Pergamum was destroyed, the games in Olympia were suppressed, the sanctuary at Didymoi was closed and the oracle of Delphi was silenced. In the course of one hundred years everything had changed, not least in the city of Ephesus. Ephesus had been the major centre of the cult of Artemis, a key fertility rite in many hellenistic cities, but Artemis was now to be supplanted not by another

goddess but by Mary the God-bearer. The council which defined Mary as 'Theotokos' in 431 was very deliberately held in
Ephesus, intending to replace one maternal-Godly icon with
another. As Christianity became established as the religion of
the empire, its icons and rituals supplanted all others. The
theological tensions that continued to emerge centred on one
crux issue: how does one relate the incarnational dynamism
of Christianity, with its love of representation and sacramental
expression, to the radical iconoclasm of the Judaic tradition
with its searing critique of all latent idolatry? There was a
growing apprehension that iconophilia was getting out of
hand and so the breaking and burning of icons began. The issues involved came to a head in the iconoclastic controversy
of the eighth century and the Second General Council of
Nicaea in 787. This, the seventh ecumenical council and the
last one accepted by the Eastern Churches, affirmed the ven-
eration of icons and crucifixes.[10] The council brought an end
to this violent internal dispute but it could do nothing about
the wonderful art that had been destroyed in this bout of
puritan theological iconoclasm. As a result, if you want to see
the early treasures of Byzantine religious art today, you will
find them in Ravenna, Italy, which survived the controversy
because of its western location whereas everything further east
was destroyed. The little that survived this convulsion within
Christianity fell to the sword of Islamic invasion in the East.
Hagia Sophia stands today in Istanbul as one of the greatest
architectural monuments of all time, a sacred space beyond
compare, yet almost devoid of its wonderful icons plundered
first by Crusaders and later by the forces of Islam. The

10. The original text of the council can be found in Denzinger-Schonmetzer,
Enchiridion Symbolorum Definitionum et Declarationum, edition XXXIII, Freiburg
im Breisgau: Herder 1965, nos. 600-601. There is an English translation in J.
Neuner and J. Dupuis eds., *The Christian Faith in the Doctrinal Documents of the
Catholic Church*, London: Collins Liturgical Publications 1983, nos. 1251-52.

Crusades began nine hundred years ago in 1095 and it is ironic to note that the first city they conquered was Nicaea, but they didn't respect the teaching of the Council of 787 as they proceeded to destroy much of the heritage of the Christian East. The internal Reformation in Western Christianity in the sixteenth century was expressed most forcibly in the iconoclastic spirit of the Reformers concerning Catholic liturgies and devotions.[11] Right down to today there is a continuing theological critique of traditional religion and all that it represents. It is as if those who are theologically literate are almost embarrassed by the manner in which people participate in what appear to be quasi-pagan rites.

This quick perusal of the history of religious iconoclasm might be summarised as follows: all monotheistic religions reject earlier religious symbols and rituals as idolatrous. In particular Judaism, Islam and Protestant Christianity, in their embrace of the Holy Word, be it the Pentateuch, the Koran or the Bible, are especially suspicious of ritual and symbolic expression. Visit a synagogue, a mosque or a Protestant church and one will see that all of the emphasis is centred on the Word, the place from which it is read is highlighted and commonly the only visual representation on the walls will be extracts from the Holy Book. There is an interesting contrast here with the traditions of the Eastern Orthodox and Western Catholic Churches with their sacramental focus on ritual and symbol. These Churches tend to incorporate earlier symbols and rituals and adapt them to the story of the new faith; in this sense they are more tactile and open to previous religious expression. In all of this, one fact is crucial – that the origins of all religious ritual are found in fertility rites. Maybe we could follow a different path than traditional theology does in its easy dismissal of these rites as idolatrous and pagan; if we

11. See, for example, Eamon Duffy, *The Stripping of the Altars: Traditional Religion in England 1400-1580*, New Haven and London: Yale University Press 1992.

look at them sympathetically we might even make important discoveries.

Fertility rites are the oldest expression of religious consciousness that we have discovered – rites intended to facilitate a good harvest, the avoidance of destructive climatic conditions, the placating of the angry gods, the fecundity of the female, the subduing of all hostile forces, the journey to the other world. All monotheistic religions characterise these fertility rites as magical and utterly reprehensible. The religious history of the Jewish people is characterised in the Hebrew Scriptures as an endless process of purification from the temptation to worship the false gods of fertility. Only through overcoming polytheism (belief in many gods) and henotheism (belief in one God amongst many others) can radical monotheism (belief that there is only one God) emerge.

Monotheism replaces rites of fertility with rites of initiation – rites through which one becomes a member of a true faith community. Further rites deepen and renew one's attachment to this community. One's identity is secure, fear is taken away and the future is safe in God's hands; thus one is liberated from all attachment to the false gods of fertility. These rites of initiation are everything – through them one is saved, without them one is lost. What constitutes these rites most of all is their vehement rejection of their pagan precursors; these must be utterly rejected in the embrace of a new faith. But is this radical distinction true?

One of the central aims of this book is to scrutinise such theological iconoclasm and to attempt to uncover its real motivation. I hope to demonstrate that the claims of theological purity are often little more than religious fundamentalism and have much more to do with cultural hegemony and political control than Christian faith. Further, they suggest that the real ground of religious belief is the life of the individual rather than the community. Such iconoclasts often believe

themselves to be intellectually and morally superior to the
pagan iconophiles in their midst, but in reality their reforms
often dull rather than enhance the life of the spirit. The arguments put forward here will not prove this hypothesis, but
much evidence will be adduced in its favour in our next chapter.

A particular example

We will close these reflections on the nature of human ritual by taking a brief look at the oldest archaeological remains
of ritual expression yet discovered in Ireland – the great megalithic passage graves in the Boyne Valley in County Meath
and at Carrowmore in County Sligo. The word 'megalith'
comes for the Greek *mega* meaning large and *lithos* meaning
stone. These huge stone constructions were put in place in
the neolithic age (coming from the Greek *neos* meaning new
or later and *lithos* meaning stone, the name given to the later
stone age) sometime in the fourth millennium before Christ.
The people who erected them were farmers living a settled life
in wooden houses. These people predated the use of metals
and naturally all of their constructions made of wood have
long since disappeared. But what is most interesting for us
was their use of stone.[12] Their public monuments were built
of stone and those that survive today, over five thousand years
later, were mainly concerned with funeral rituals and ancestor
worship. Huge boulders and stone slabs were moved into
place in order to create these monuments. As you travel
through the Irish countryside you will see dolmens, court-
cairns and passage graves. The really interesting question is –
why did they do it?

We have already noted that every civilisation tries to bring
order into the disorder of the world, tries to establish cosmos
in the midst of chaos. One of the great examples of this is the

12. See Jean-Pierre Mohen, *The World of Megaliths*, New York: Facts on File
1990, pp. 86-87.

search for permanence and continuity in the context of the transitory nature of human life and experience. For these people stone was permanent, solid, certain; it was a way of keeping in contact with the ancestors who had disappeared and, particularly when associated with the rhythmic constancy of the lunar and solar cycles or the mysterious otherness of the mountain top, it surely became the focus for ritual expression. We do not know in any precise way in what sort of rituals these people participated but we can draw some tentative ideas together. One could simply dismiss these people as deranged fools who had too much time on their hands, but such arrogance beggars belief. Look at what they did. In Carrowmore they built one of the biggest megalithic grave systems in the world between the two wonderfully mysterious mountains of Knocknarea and Ben Bulbin. Mountain tops were amongst the most important symbols in archaic cultures, the place where heaven and earth embraced and divine power and vision were most readily accessible. One could dismiss Knocknarea and Ben Bulbin as nothing more than large hills rising to 1,073 feet (327 metres) and 1,726 feet (526 metres) respectively, with none of the grandeur of the great mountain tops. In Irish folklore and mythology, however, these are indeed great mountains, places redolent of mysterious figures, gigantic feats and stunning panoramas over land, lake and sea. In the plain between these mountains neolithic inhabitants buried their dead with what must have been extraordinary rituals, given the enormous effort that the erection of these stone edifices would have required. The very act of formal burial was one of the most important developments in the history of ritual. Corpses were no longer left in ditches or abandoned to the mercy of wild animals. Instead they became the focus for rites of passage which opened the doors of the other world.

It is of course the startlingly interesting neolithic passage grave at Newgrange in the Boyne Valley that attracts most comment concerning archaic ritual forms in Ireland. A long passage opens into an inner chamber which is flooded with sunlight from the rising sun of the winter solstice through an opening over the lintel of the door at the entry point to the passage. The winter solstice was a classic threshold experience. Mircea Eliade comments:

> Indeed, throughout the north, the gradual shortening of the days as the winter solstice approaches inspires fear that the sun may die away completely ... the falling or the darkening of the sun becomes one of the signs of the coming end of the world, of the conclusion, that is, of one cosmic cycle.[13]

In Newgrange these neolithic people ritualised one of the key liminal moments of the year and brought it together with one of the key liminal moments in life – the experience of death. Thus they ritualised two types of death, the death of the sun and the death of human beings whose bodily remains, maybe after cremation, journeyed up the passage to the beginning of the other world. And as they awaited the rebirth of the sun in the days of spring, so too the dead were endlessly reborn through ancestor worship. Imagine their sense of *communitas* with the dead, the cosmos, the sun. Brendan Purcell comments:

> Here, at the centre of the world where heaven, earth and underworld intersect, the Boyne people expressed their experience of the mysterious answer to their search for participation in everlasting order. Here they applied all their artistic, technological, astronomic and measuring skills to elevate midwinter sunrise into a cosmic YES between sun and earth at the zero point of their mutual forsakenness. After the longest night of the year, at sunrise on the short-

13. Mircea Eliade, *Patterns in Comparative Religion*, London: Sheed and Ward 1958, p. 149.

est day, the direct rays of the sun burst through the narrow roof-box over the entrance, along the winding passage, to the inner chamber, which explodes into light for nearly twenty minutes. Cutting through the heart of all reality, when darkness seems to have finally enveloped the world, light shines. At the time when sun and earth seem closest to the condition of death, the promise of a new year of life dawns for both of them.[14]

As the sun crept up the passage it surely awoke a sense of hope and life even on the darkest and dreariest of days; amidst all the contingencies of life, here was a reality that was simultaneously permanent and changing; the old sun was fading away but at its moment of death it was reborn anew. So too with human life – as it underwent its passage through death, the light would not be quenched.

It is easy to dismiss the rituals of Carrowmore and Newgrange, whatever precisely they were, as amounting to nothing more than archaic fertility rites. In terms of modern categories this is precisely what they were. But later monotheistic believers should be slow to dismiss earlier systems of ritual and belief since it is on the shoulders of these archaic traditions that religions grow and develop. This is particularly true in Ireland and other Celtic lands. When the Celts swept into these lands fifteen hundred years or so after the end of the neolithic civilisations, they appear to have easily assimilated the remains of these earlier cultures in a new synthesis. Similarly Christianity evolved in Ireland in a Celtic environment seemingly without bloodshed; the first Irish martyrs are not found until Reformation times whereas earlier Irish saints were heroic figures like those found in early mythologies. In other words, one religious system seems to have superimposed itself upon another in Irish religious history without any great difficulty,

14. Brendan Purcell, 'In Search of Newgrange: Long Night's Journey Into Day' in Richard Kearney ed., *The Irish Mind*, Dublin: Wolfhound Press 1985, pp. 46-48.

and so we are the inheritors of a rich amalgam of symbols, rituals and stories which evolved over several millennia. However, since the Reformation, the evolution of religious ritual, symbol and story in Ireland has been marked by violence, fierce theological controversies and deepening divisions. The history of religious rituals in Ireland is particularly interesting given the earlier evolutionary developments and the later revolutionary divisions. Given that the best way to study and understand the nature of ritual is detailed analysis of a particular example, we will turn our attention in the next chapter to further dimensions of the Irish context.

The Irish Context[1]

MICHAEL: *But there is one memory of that Lughnasa time that visits me most often ... In that memory atmosphere is more real than incident and everything is simultaneously actual and illusory ... When I remember it I think of it as dancing. Dancing with eyes half closed because to open them would break the spell. Dancing as if language had surrendered to movement – as if this ritual, this wordless ceremony, was now the way to speak, to whisper private and sacred things, to be in touch with some otherness. Dancing as if the heart of life and all its hopes might be found in those assuaging notes and those hushed rhythms and in those silent and hypnotic movements. Dancing as if language no longer existed because words were no longer necessary ...*

Brian Friel, *Dancing at Lughnasa*

One of the key emphases of contemporary theology is context. With the importance now attached to hermeneutics and given the decontextualised nature of earlier theologies, theologians today clearly write and want to write from differing perspectives. Black, feminist, liberation, Asian, African and

1. Some of the material used in this chapter has been published in 'Irish Catholics: A People Formed By Ritual' in Eoin G. Cassidy ed., *Faith and Culture in the Irish Context*, Dublin: Veritas 1996, pp. 83-99; and in 'The Meaning of Pilgrimage' in Donal Flanagan ed., *The Meaning of Knock*, Dublin: Columba Press 1997, pp. 55-70. An earlier draft of this chapter entitled 'The Great Hunger: Shaping Irish Catholicism' was read to the Irish Theological Association, 21 January 1995, and to a colloquium on the Irish famine held in the Irish College, Rome, 4-5 May 1996.

political theologies exist and thrive. Though doing theology in differing contexts, most of these theologians are highly critical of the traditional academy-centred theology of Europe. The great temptation of the latter was to understand itself as the only context in which one could validly do theology.

Isn't it interesting that one adjective which seems unreal before the word 'theology' is 'Irish'? Why has an Irish theology not emerged? Given the importance of religion in Irish society, the conflict in Northern Ireland with its religious overtones, and the long history of Christianity in Ireland, one would imagine that there are few more fertile contexts for doing theology. Yet it is only in recent years that one could speak of the beginning of an 'Irish theology'. One of the reasons why it took so long to emerge is the overwhelming animosity between Catholics and Protestants which is so characteristic of modern Irish history. Such animosity was the key context of Irish theology from the Reformation through to the 1960s. Only when one leaves aside the context of the Reformation debates can other plausible contexts for constructing an Irish theology effectively emerge. This chapter is an effort to establish one such context – the historical and contemporary significance of traditional religion amongst Irish Catholics.

What is this traditional religion? One could use other adjectives such as 'folk' or 'popular' to describe it but these terms give rise to pejorative interpretations. When people speak of popular, folk religion they often intend to contrast this with mainstream monotheistic 'true' religion, the latter functioning as a purifier of the insidious idolatry of the former. When I refer to traditional religion I mean that matrix of beliefs, practices, rituals and customs that constitutes a living incarnate religion. Such a religion functions in a very practical way as an interpretative model of human existence and brings together in an apparently 'unholy alliance' the residue of archaic fertility rites, land-based rituals, orthodox Christian beliefs and a broad notion of the sacramentality of life. There is much in the traditional practices of Irish Catholics that has not been integrated into any coherent theological framework; just think of fairy forts, holy wells, bonfire nights, ghost stories, pilgrimages, patterns, wakes. All of the latter have constituted rich data for folklorists, artists and anthropologists but have been largely ignored by theologians. This chapter is an effort to enter into conversation with the past in order to textualise our present experience.

When one applies the insights of Turner and van Gennep to the history of religions, the distinction between rites of fertility and rites of initiation is not nearly so clear-cut as religious iconoclasts would have us believe. The true distinction is more likely between rites that renew identity and completely decadent magical rites that enslave the human person. I would like to argue that amongst Irish Catholics rites associated with the fertility of the land co-existed with rites of initiation. Christian and pre-Christian elements had been fused over centuries, so powerfully enmeshed in Irish Catholic consciousness that they seem to have survived completely intact the theological iconoclasm of the Reformation, with its searing critique of image, symbol and ritual. The first half of the nineteenth century in Ireland saw the emergence of a serious Anglican evangelical programme and its Catholic response with the full weight of the Counter-Reformation being unleashed in Ireland for the first time. Both of these tendencies capitalised on the Great Hunger of 1845-48 in their desire to further their basic goal of purifying Irish Catholics of their quasi-pagan instincts. An analysis of two traditional rituals will demonstrate what I mean; they are the festival of *Lughnasa* and the pilgrimage to St Patrick's Purgatory on Lough Derg.

The Festival of Lughnasa

Maire MacNeill's work, *The Festival of Lughnasa,* first published in 1962, is an outstanding contribution to recent Irish folk history.[2] Drawing from many different sources, not least folk memory, she pieces together what was one of the great rituals of Irish life. There were four great festivals in the old Irish Celtic year: *Samhain* (November 1st), *Imbolg* (February 1st), *Bealtaine* (May 1st) and *Lughnasa* (August 1st).[3] It is interesting to note the dates of these four festivals; they exactly bisect the dates of the four solar solstices. Thus *Samhain* falls mid-way between 21 September and 21 December, *Imbolg* similarly mid-way between 21 December and 21 March, *Bealtaine* is mid-way between 21 March and 21 June and, finally, *Lughnasa* comes mid-way between 21 June and 21 September. *Samhain* was the festival of the disappearing sun and the other world; the dead returned to visit their people and strange powers were active. This was also the beginning of a new year. *Imbolg* was the festival of springtime celebrating the start of tilling, the birth of lambs and the return of fishermen to the sea. *Bealtaine* was a festival centring on the goddess, imploring her to take care of the cattle now returning to pasture. There were prayers and blessings galore to protect the animals and to intercede for a good harvest later in the year. These three festivals became associated in the Christian calendar with the dead, St Brigid and Mary. But the fourth great festival, that of *Lughnasa,* was not incorporated into the Christian calendar. Slowly but surely it was suppressed and it is only recently, with the work of Maire MacNeill and Brian Friel,[4] that the meaning of this festival has been retrieved. The *nasad* (games or assembly) of the god Lugh was a celebra-

2. Maire MacNeill, *The Festival of Lughnasa,* University College Dublin: Comhairle Bhéaloideas Éireann 1982. (First published in 1962.)

3. See M. MacNeill, *The Festival of Lughnasa,* p. 1.

4. Brian Friel, *Dancing at Lughnasa,* London: Faber and Faber 1990.

tion of plenty, an offering of the first fruits of the harvest, the overcoming of hunger. The first fruits were there for all to see in the last days of July and the first days of August; there was new corn and new potatoes, the earth was yielding its fruit and there was much to celebrate. The fears of *Bealtaine* concerning the cow and dairy production, and of mid-summer's day (21 June) with its fear of the crops failing to come to maturity, had passed. The hungry month of July, hungry because the remains of the previous year's harvest were probably already consumed, was over and the celebration could begin. People gathered on heights and at springs, they

> made the customary rounds, picked bilberries and wild flowers, danced, played and fell in love, raced and wrestled, competed in tests of strength and agility, joined in the routine fights, met old friends and exchanged news, heard old stories from the elders and grew to know the landmarks.[5]

They celebrated the land as they looked out over its mysterious beauty. This was truly a festival of the first fruits of the harvest.

In the eighteenth and nineteenth centuries the festival of *Lughnasa,* then known by a variety of names – *Domhnach Chrom Dubh,* Bilberry Sunday, Garland Sunday, etc. – was celebrated on the last Sunday of July (as it is to this day insofar as it is celebrated at all). It was still a festival of first fruits, not now the first sheaf of corn nor the slaughter of a lamb, but the first digging of the new potatoes. Potatoes had been introduced into Ireland in the sixteenth century. Yielding four times as much carbohydrate per acre as wheat, this South American import spread rapidly after its arrival – first in gardens and small farms, then as a key field crop after 1700. Corn had all but disappeared in the west of the country by the mid-nineteenth century. The new potatoes were dug at the end of

5. M. MacNeill, *The Festival at Lughnasa,* p. 428.

July and the occasion was marked by ritual observance and boisterous celebration. Even in the homes of the poorest cottiers this was a special day, marked by a feast of mashed new potatoes with milk and seasoned with cabbage or onions, known variously as *ceallaigh,* cally, colcannon, *brúightín,* bruisy or poundy. People went to the old *Lughnasa* sites to do the 'rounds'[6] and to say their prayers. The festival commemorated and ensured the routing of the blight, the harvest was beginning and the first fruits were being celebrated. Maire MacNeill comments:

> it was the day when the sickle was first put to the ripened corn, as in later times it became the day when the spade turned up the first meal of potatoes. To that simple core much solemnity was added, and a great body of myth and ceremonial and popular custom accrued. Underneath it all the consciousness remained of its essential character, perhaps nowhere so succinctly expressed as in the simple and ringing words of an old woman of the Ballinrobe district speaking of the day known locally as Domhnach Chrom Dubh, 'The harvest is in and the hunger is over!'[7]

Christianity did incorporate aspects of the feast into its rituals while most of the features repugnant to Christian belief were suppressed, with the exception of faction fighting. Lugh was replaced by Patrick, the gatherings became pilgrimages (especially to holy wells), prayers were recited as one did the rounds of the stone or hill or well. Patrick had the same powers as Lugh – to protect the crops, to lend importance to a certain place, to overcome the forces of evil. The gatherings in each place developed a link with a particular saint and became known as 'patterns' or 'patrons'. Yet the clergy never ceased in

6. The 'rounds' refers to the ancient Irish ritual practice of walking around the sacred place, be it a church or a ruin or a graveyard or a saint's bed, reciting verbal prayers.

7. M. MacNeill, *The Festival at Lughnasa*, p. 66.

their struggle to suppress these traditional gatherings. Archdeacon T. O'Rorke, commenting on a *Lughnasa* festival in Ballysadare, Co Sligo, states:

> The priests of the parish and of the neighbourhood left no effort untried to put an end to these excesses ... In 1826 the clergy exerted themselves more than on any former occasion, but they laboured in vain, and in spite of all their preachings and supplications, the patron of that year was the most numerous and probably the most unruly ever held ... The tents were full of guzzlers; the itinerant dealers sold out their poteen and gingerbread as fast as they could receive the price; dancing circles whirled here and there around pipers and fiddlers; ballad singers ... drawled out their doleful ditties on highway robbery and murder; mountebanks, sleight-of-hand men, and card-sharpers performed their feats and tricks so as to engross the attention of the gaping rustic ... drunken men staggered and shouted, and flourished their shillelaghs; excited men moved about in knots and groups preparing for the fight of the night; ... it was a very Babel of noises.[8]

Despite the best efforts of the various Christian denominations and the State apparatus, the people clung to their archaic ritual celebrations which probably dated back more than two thousand years. But the famine of the 1840s was to change all of that.

The Pilgrimage to Lough Derg

This archaic pilgrimage has strong roots in pre-Christian traditions. Known as the Red Lake *(Loch Dearg)* it is associated in folklore with Patrick's destruction of evil forces and the spilling of their blood.[9] This motif of pain, struggle and hardship flows through Irish history and is particularly emphasised

8. M. MacNeill, *The Festival at Lughnasa*, p. 115-16.
9. See M. MacNeill, *The Festival at Lughnasa*, p. 505 and p. 531.

in pilgrimage. Pilgrims went to a distant island where barefoot they fasted, prayed and went without sleep. Lough Derg was never a place of magic for the Irish but rather an instance of true liminal encounter. The liminality was obvious: an island, on a barren lake, towards the northwest corner of Ireland, in the northwest corner of Europe, falling off into the setting sun. Here one's identity was renewed through *communitas* where the distinctions and hierarchies of society were abrogated in the barefoot, sleepless, hungry and utterly realistic interaction with the physical world. Like the festival of *Lughnasa* and other 'patterns', one did the rounds reciting one's prayers. Hunger and discomfort were embraced as all too real in the lives of this people. Lough Derg was far more than a pious exercise, than a mock identification with the *Via Crucis* – it was an encounter with some of the deepest truths about life. For medieval visitors from Europe it was a romantic, magical, curative place, but for the Irish it was, as Victor Turner says, 'like a vertical shaft driven into the past, disclosing deep strata of ancient symbols, potent signifiers ... which reinforce nationalistic sentiments'.[10] The forces of church and State made many efforts to close St Patrick's Purgatory on Lough Derg but the people continued to assemble in this hallowed place to celebrate and renew their identity.

> Far from being an opiate for the people Lough Derg and other pilgrimage shrines in Ireland ... may have kept alive the cultural basis for national political struggle, providing it with its root paradigm: that martyrdom should be embraced, if necessary, for the good of the people.[11]

It's interesting to note that the highest recorded number of pilgrims to Lough Derg in one year was 30,000 in 1846, 1,300

10. Victor Turner and Edith Turner, *Image and Pilgrimage in Christian Culture*, p. 106.
11. Victor Turner and Edith Turner, *Image and Pilgrimage ...*, pp. 136-37.

on one day alone.[12] Tragically, over the succeeding few years the pain of Lough Derg would be as nothing compared to the pain of hunger.

The festival of *Lughnasa* and the pilgrimage to Lough Derg are just two examples of many that one could choose to analyse in traditional Irish religion. They both involved separation from ordinary life and a very definite liminal/*communitas* experience. The people went to the holy well or up the mountain or over to the island and there, at the edge of things, they rediscovered their communion with each other, with the earth, with the first fruits of the harvest, with the past, with pain, with human frailty, with the dead. And then they returned, they reaggregated into ordinary life. Isn't it interesting that the retrieval of this liminal/*communitas* encounter in contemporary Irish consciousness is found in the work of poets, artists and playrights and seems near completely absent in the work of theologians? Seamus Heaney's *Station Island* [13] and Brian Friel's *Dancing at Lughnasa*[14] are outstanding contributions to re-imagining traditional Irish religion as these authors go to the margins of their own experience in order to revisit the liminal spaces that their forebears often inhabited. Irish churches and theologians have been slow to visit these wellsprings, mainly because of the events of the 1840s and their repercussions.

The Great Hunger and Its Aftermath

One of the greatest disasters in the peacetime history of the world was the Irish famine of the 1840s, traditionally called the Great Hunger.[15] It is difficult to overstate the hor-

---

12. Victor Turner and Edith Turner, *Image and Pilgrimage ...*, p. 259.
13. Seamus Heaney, *Station Island*, London: Faber and Faber 1984.
14. See note no 4.
15. I have analysed the effects of this famine on later Irish Catholicism in 'Irish Catholics: A People Formed By Ritual' in Eoin G. Cassidy ed., *Faith and Culture in the Irish Context*, Dublin: Veritas 1996, pp. 83-99.

ror that unfolded. Statistics are always bland and cold; one must remember that behind each statistic stands a human person. The population of the island fell from approximately 8.5 millions in 1846 to about 6.5 millions in 1851.[16] One million people died and at least another million emigrated. The worst affected region was the province of Connacht (which is made up of counties Galway, Leitrim, Mayo, Roscommon and Sligo), where in five years the population dropped from roughly 1.5 millions to one million.[17] This was disaster on a scale seldom, if ever, encountered before. Over a short few years the world of Irish cottiers and farm labourers ruptured and died; there were no new potatoes to celebrate at *Lughnasa* time and the hardship of Lough Derg paled in comparison to the pain of famine. As, centuries previously, the Black Death had changed the religious consciousness of Europe, so too the religious mind and heart of the Irish peasantry would be transformed. In this sense it is probably true to speak of contemporary Irish Catholicism as a post-famine phenomenon. In the aftermath of the famine there was a relentless attack on traditional rituals and, as Eamon Duffy comments on the similar iconoclasm of the Reformation in England, the attack on them 'was an attempt to redefine the boundaries of human community and, in an act of exorcism, to limit the claims of the past, and the people of the past, on the people of the present'.[18] The cataclysm of the Great Hunger of the 1840s was just such a possibility for exorcism and there was no shortage of Protestant and Catholic exorcists. The famine changed everything and facilitated the emergence of that pious indi-

16. The census of 1841 measured the Irish population as 8,175,125; in 1851 it was 6,552,385. But the population was rising in the early 1840s and had probably reached 8.5 millions by 1846.

17. The population of Connacht in 1841 was 1,418,859; in 1851 it had dropped to 1,010,031. As in the rest of the country the population was rising in the early 1840s and had probably reached 1.5 millions by 1846.

18. Eamon Duffy, *The Stripping of the Altars*, p. 8.

vidualism which is so characteristic of late nineteenth and twentieth century Christianity.

Anglican evangelicals and the majority of Catholic priests had one thing in common in the first half of the nineteenth century – to convert this people with their predilection for pagan rites to true Christianity. The iconoclasm of Protestant evangelicals with regard to the Irish folk traditions was clearcut. Here was a quasi-pagan people placating superstitious gods and seeking to earn salvation. The comments of Rev Henry M'Manus, a presbyterian missionary who was in the Joyce country of the Maumturk mountains in July 1841, are typical. Having described a Mass that was celebrated, he goes on to say:

> This worship was followed by a sudden transition, characteristic in all ages, of the religion which man himself originates, and which he loves. Amusement became the order of the day. The pipers struck up their merry tunes in the tents, and the dancing began ... Bread and cakes were abundantly supplied by pedlars and whiskey flowed on all sides. Under such circumstances we may conceive the uproarious hilarity of an excitable people. Nor did it all cease till the Sabbath sun sought the western wave.[19]

Suggestions of cultural superiority were common amongst Protestant commentators. Yet what was really significant was the perceived effort to convert the Irish poor through what came to be known as the 'New Reformation'.[20] Relationships between Anglicans and Catholics deteriorated noticeably from the 1820s onwards: Catholics in Ireland believed that a new proselytising zeal was evident amongst Anglican evangelicals whilst a resurgent Catholicism in England sowed fear in the hearts of many Irish Protestants. These tensions ultimately

19. M. MacNeill, *The Festival at Lughnasa*, p. 126.
20. See Donal Kerr, *'A Nation of Beggars'? Priests, People, and Politics in Famine Ireland 1846-52*, Oxford: Clarendon Press 1994, pp. 206 and 324.

found their focus in the famine controversy over 'souperism', the claim that Anglican evangelicals distributed soup to impoverished Catholics on condition that they converted to Anglicanism and sent their children to what was effectively the equivalent of Sunday School. People who 'took the soup' became known as 'soupers' and later Irish Catholic tradition used this term to identify those who had apostasised and to highlight the great Catholic triumph in convincing most adherents not to 'take the soup'. That a very significant number of Anglican evangelicals indulged in this grotesque form of proselytism is unquestionably true; that some Irish Anglican pastors abhorred the practice is equally true.[21] The guilty included Thomas Plunkett, Bishop of the united dioceses of Tuam, Killala and Achonry, Alexander R. C. Dallas, founder of the Society for Irish Church Missions, and Edward Nangle who set up a Protestant colony in Achill. Their actions, particularly in Co Mayo, were abhorrent and were well summarised by Dallas himself when he wrote that his movement 'was nurtured in blood'. He added that:

> the awful famine of 1847, with its attendant horrors in 1848 worked wonderfully for its development. Thus it might almost be said that the movement gave a character to the famine rather than the famine characterised the movement.[22]

Understandably, Catholic leaders responded aggressively to what they perceived to be a Second Reformation; Tobias Kirby advised the bishops 'to repress any efforts of the Protestants who give the poor a morsel of bread with one

21. These issues are analysed in two works by Desmond Bowen, *Souperism: Myth or Reality, A Study of Catholics and Protestants during the Great Famine*, Cork: Mercier Press 1970, and *The Protestant Crusade in Ireland 1800-70*, Dublin: Gill and Macmillan 1978. For a very different perspective on the reality of 'souperism' see, Irene Whelan, 'The Stigma of Souperism' in Cathal Póirtéir ed., *The Great Irish Famine*, Cork: Mercier Press 1995, pp. 135-154.
22. Quoted in D. Bowen, *Souperism: Myth or Reality*, p. 127.

hand and kill their immortal souls with the other'.[23] As before, a Reformation would be met head on with a Counter-
Reformation.

The leader of this Counter-Reformation was Paul Cullen.
The noted historian, Donal A. Kerr, comments that 'for
Cullen, countering Protestant proselytism was a priority and
his hatred of it is crucial to an understanding of his policy in
his early years in Ireland'.[24] The effect of Cullen on the post-
famine church was enormous. In a famous article, Emmet
Larkin describes the changes that occurred as amounting to a
'devotional revolution'.[25] The most powerful expression of
this 'revolution' was probably found in the parish mission
which seemed to make an almost indelible mark on participants. The missioners – Vincentians, Redemptorists, Jesuits –
came from abroad to inculcate renewed theological emphases:

> for instance, the decided dualism of salvation theology, the
> heavy reliance on sacrament and sacramental to underpin
> evangelisation, the primacy of confession in pastoral strat-
> egy, the defensive stance of ecclesiology, the weaning of the
> people from an over-reliance on elements of folk religion
> to a chapel-centred practice of faith.[26]

The latter was all important because, as a result of the suppres-
sion of the monasteries and church buildings under Henry VIII
in the mid-sixteenth century, and the continuing legal hostility
to Catholicism right through to the early nineteenth century,

23. Quoted in D. Bowen, *Souperism: Myth or Reality*, p. 143. Tobias Kirby was
Cullen's successor as Rector of the Irish College in Rome.
24. Donal A. Kerr, *'A Nation of Beggars'?*, p. 324.
25. See Emmet Larkin, 'The Devotional Revolution in Ireland' in *American
Historical Review*, 1972 vol. 87, pp. 625-652. Also published in E. Larkin, *The
Historical Dimensions of Irish Catholicism*, Washington DC: Catholic University
of America Press 1984, pp. 57-89.
26. M. Baily, 'The Parish Mission Apostolate of the Redemptorists in Ireland,
1851-1898' in R. Gallagher and B. McConvery eds., *History and Conscience: Studies
in Honour of Sean O'Riordan CSsR*, Dublin: Gill and Macmillan 1989, p. 275.

there was a paucity of church buildings in Ireland. The first half of the nineteenth century saw an explosion in the building of chapels with maybe as many as one thousand new constructions. The key pastoral goal of Archbishop Cullen was to turn Irish Catholics into a chapel-going population. He achieved this aim through insisting that Mass be offered only in chapels. Station Masses were frowned upon.[27] The traditional ritual of the funeral wake was undermined by removing corpses from homes to chapels. Many other traditional practices were suppressed and replaced with chapel-centred imports such as 'forty hours, perpetual adoration, novenas, blessed altars, *Via Crucis,* benediction, vespers, devotion to the Sacred Heart and the Immaculate Conception, jubilees, triduums, pilgrimages, shrines, processions and retreats'.[28] Groups emerged to promote participation in these exercises: confraternities, sodalities, Children of Mary, altar and temperance societies. 'These public exercises were also reinforced by the use of devotional tools and aids: beads, scapulars, medals, missals, prayer books, catechisms and holy pictures.'[29] By 1870 the Cullen reforms were triumphant. The census returns of 1861 proved that the efforts of Protestant proselytisers were essentially a failure and the 'great mass of the Irish people became practising Catholics, which they have uniquely and essentially remained both at home and abroad down to the present day'.[30]

As usual, this revolution/evolution was iconophile with regard to its new practices and radically iconoclast concerning folk traditions. Just look at the impact on the traditional rituals

27. Because of the penal laws the practice had evolved of the priest travelling around from one townland to another in order to offer Mass. These Masses often took place in ordinary homes and were called station Masses.

28. E. Larkin, *The Historical Dimensions of Irish Catholicism,* pp. 77-78.

29. E. Larkin, *The Historical Dimensions of Irish Catholicism,* p. 78.

30. E. Larkin, *The Historical Dimensions of Irish Catholicism,* p. 58.

that we analysed earlier. Pilgrimages to holy wells, even at
Lughnasa time, continued but they had nothing to do with
the celebration of first fruits; commonly they were portrayed
as temperance gatherings. The rounds were made but there
were no festivities. The ancient ascetic spirit, so well manifested
in the pilgrimages to Croagh Patrick and Lough Derg, was reduced to little more than atonement for sexual sins. In the
context of famine it wasn't difficult to link sexual behaviour,
guilt, sin and death in the minds of these people for, all too
obviously, there had been too many mouths to feed. The spirit
of the people was broken by the famine and the new spirituality assumed the high moral ground of the respectable middle-
class, rejecting the raucous religion of an earlier time in the
embrace of individual rigour, personal scrupulosity and sexual
abstinence. Nowhere was this spirit more manifest than in the
great symbol of post-famine Irish Catholicism – the sacrament of confession. Donal A. Kerr comments:

> the cluster of beliefs and practices that constituted the reli-
> gion of the poorer peasants, in addition to such central
> Catholic devotions as the sacraments, the rosary, fasting
> and daily prayers, also included devotions connected with
> patterns, pilgrimages, holy wells, wakes and charms. Many
> of these came under attack, as a reforming church opposed
> them as either superstitious or providing the occasion for
> insobriety, immorality, or other abuses. The Famine dealt
> them a devastating blow, for it bore heaviest on the labour-
> ing and cottier classes. Thenceforth, religious practices be-
> came more 'orthodox' and the quickening pace at which
> this took place wrought a rapid change in Irish devotional
> life.[31]

And yet the change was not complete. The exorcism failed to
banish all the ancient archetypes. Despite the unleashing of

31. D. Kerr, *'A Nation of Beggars'*, pp. 318-19.

massive iconoclastic forces in the midst of a society in disarray, where death and emigration stalked the land and the language of the people faced near terminal decline, this effort to redefine the boundaries of human community by banishing so many traditions could not ultimately succeed. The one thing it could not control was the imagination and its capacity to revisit these ancient wellsprings. Cullen's reforms crept westwards through the country slowly but surely. Yet they never managed to completely extinguish the old traditions. One hundred and fifty years later we can inhabit the same spaces as our forebears at station Masses, funeral wakes, patterns, holy wells and pilgrimages. But with what type of consciousness do we enter these sacred spaces? As Thomas G. McGrath comments:

> Do we acknowledge a valid role for popular religion or do we look on the venerable devotions of popular religion, with their now seemingly incongruous mixture of the sacred and the profane, as merely superstitions or as evidence that these people were not practising Catholics at all? To do so would be a condescending dismissal and a dangerous misreading of the vibrant heritage of Irish Catholicism.[32]

That heritage deserves a serious theological interpretation. How can we use modern scholarship to look again at what was happening in Ireland in the middle of the nineteenth century? I would like to draw from several different strands of thought in order to demonstrate that the religious iconoclasm which attacked the traditional rituals of the people was and is theologically questionable and has more to do with political control and cultural hegemony than with Christian faith.

32. Thomas G. McGrath, 'The Tridentine Evolution of Modern Irish Catholicism, 1563-1962: A Re-examination of the "Devotional Revolution" Thesis' in R. Ó Muirí ed., *Irish Church History Today*, Cumann Seanchais Ard Mhaca, 10 March 1990, p. 98.

(1) The interpretation of the Letter to the Galatians

It might seem strange at this stage to turn the clock back to one of the earliest pieces of Christian writing, but what was happening in Galatia in the middle of the first century is particularly instructive for our reflections. As a result of the initial missionary outreach of the early Christian church, a Christian community was established in Galatia. Clearly many of the members of this community were Gentiles who had embraced the new faith and who had received the gift of the Spirit. But before long, Judaisers, those who claimed that one could not accept Jesus as Messiah and saviour unless one embraced the central tenets of Judaism, arrived on the scene demanding that the Gentile Galatians be circumcised, abstain from unclean foods and observe the rituals and festivals demanded by the Torah if they were to become true Christians. This is the controversy which Paul's Letter to the Galatians addresses. For centuries readers have interpreted his message as a rejection of all rituals and customs whether they be those of the Jews or of Gentile converts. However, as we will now see, there is another way of interpreting Paul's theological outlook in this letter.

Nobody more than St Paul has been used to condemn pagan practices throughout history. One finds in Paul, especially in the letters to the Romans and the Galatians, a rejection of all empty human works in the embrace of a new faith. Surely here we have one of the great iconoclasts of all time, with his emphasis on justification by faith. But Paul clearly adopted different approaches at different times to the varied cultural/religious systems that he encountered. One can contrast for instance his rejection of the cult of Diana (Artemis) in Ephesus (see Acts 19:23-41) with his much more nuanced approach on the Areopagus in Athens (Acts 17:19-34). It is only with the Protestant Reformation in the sixteenth century that one gets the extraordinary emphasis on the salvation of the individual as being the core theological insight of Paul's letters. In fact, this Lutheran interpretation became so dominant that there didn't really seem to be any other way to read Paul except through the lens of a sense of one's own personal sinfulness opening the way to justification by faith. No doubt such an interpretation would have spurred on the proselytising evangelicals who were active in Ireland in the nineteenth century to denounce zealously all traditional customs and rituals as pathetic expressions of a sinful spirit. The Letter to the Galatians surely proves, as history has led us to believe, that all human works and rites are valueless since faith in Christ alone will justify us. Even the rituals and laws of God's own people – circumcision, dietary laws, Sabbath observance – are not necessary for salvation. The process of evangelisation is the process of purification of these false hopes so that one sets one's heart on Christ alone.

Traditionally the Letter to the Galatians has been interpreted as concerning the salvation of the individual sinner. But much recent scholarship gives us a very different picture in its claim that Paul's primary concern was not the salvation of the individual sinner but rather the cultural rights of Gentiles. K. Stendahl comments:

> A doctrine of justification by faith was hammered out by Paul for the very specific and limited purpose of defending the rights of Gentile converts to be full and genuine heirs to the promises of God to Israel ... This was Paul's very special stance, and he defended it zealously against any compromise that required circumcision or the keeping of kosher food laws by Gentile Christians ... In none of his writings does he give us information about what he thought to be proper in these matters for Jewish Christians. Himself a Jew, but with a special mission to the Gentiles, Paul is never heard to urge Jewish Christians to live like him in these respects ... When he rebukes Peter in

Antioch, it is not for Peter's practice of keeping a kosher table but for Peter's changing his attitudes under pressure from Jerusalem ... In respect to his defence of the rights and the freedom of Gentile converts, Paul has provided ample and full documentation in Galatians.[33]

This alternative interpretation is also supported by the work of E. P. Sanders and F. J. Matera.[34] In this interpretation, Galatians refers not to the justification of the individual but to the cultural rights of Gentiles who become Christians. They do not have to renounce their own customs and embrace those of the Jewish Christians, just as the Jews do not renounce their customs on becoming Christian. With the radical iconoclasm of Judaism concerning all other ethnic/religious systems, it was almost inevitable that the early Jewish Christians would couple Christian faith with their Jewish traditions. Paul rejected this.

While the traditional interpretation views Paul as combating a righteousness by works that seeks to assure one's own salvation, this view of Galatians argues that the legalism which Paul opposes is a cultural hegemony rather than a legalistic morality. To put it anachronistically, the Judaisers or agitators have come to Galatia and have said, 'In order to become a Christian, you must first become a Jew!' Thus the Gentiles must abandon the customs and practices of their culture and adopt those of Judaism in order to be counted as full members of the church.[35]

Looked at in reverse, Paul's argument is obvious: the Jews are not compelled to surrender their cultural traditions on be-

33. Krister Stendahl, *Paul Among Jews and Christians*, Philadelphia: Fortress Press 1976, p. 2.
34. E. P. Sanders, *Paul, the Law and the Jewish People*, London: SCM Press 1985; F. J. Matera, *Galatians, Sacra Pagina Series Volume 9*, Collegeville: The Liturgical Press 1992.
35. F. J. Matera, *Galatians*, pp. 29-30.

coming Christian even though these are in no sense necessary
for salvation. Nowhere in Paul's writings does he demand that
the Jews abandon their hallowed traditions even though he
ceaselessly points out that they are not necessary for salvation.
Why then would he demand otherwise of the Gentiles? And
here's a little irony: the Galatians were a Celtic people! Why
indeed should we ask the Celts to renounce their ways?

> The subject of Galatians is not whether or not humans,
> abstractly conceived, can by good deeds earn enough merit
> to be declared righteous at the judgment; it is the condi-
> tion on which Gentiles enter the people of God.[36]

That condition is faith in Christ, which does not imply that
they embrace the cultural traditions of the Jews nor that they
must renounce their own. Such is the freedom that the gospel
bestows. This was one of the first great lessons learned by the
Christian Church but one that has often been forgotten
throughout its history.

Yet surely it is the case that some rituals and traditions must
be rejected by Christians? Of course this is true but one needs
to be very careful here, as Paul was, that one's primary interest
is Christian faith and not any form of cultural hegemony. We
will now turn to the work of a leading contemporary theologian to help us analyse this question more precisely.

(2) The liberation theology of Juan Luis Segundo

Juan Luis Segundo was an important contributor in developing what has come to be known as 'liberation theology'.
The key change that liberation theology introduced into the
discipline of theology was a renewed emphasis on methodology.
Liberation theologians are very critical of what they perceive
to be the academic irrelevance and oppressive tone of much
traditional theology. This, they believe, is in large part due to
the method deployed. Theologians have traditionally ap-

36. E. P. Sanders, *Paul, the Law and the Jewish People*, p. 18.

proached questions concerning God, Jesus of Nazareth, just-ice, poverty, the interpretation of scripture, church and sacra-ment, in a detached academic manner rather than from the perspective of lived human experience. One must surely ac-knowledge that people have different experiences and that these give rise to differing theological judgments. The human experience that the liberation theologians want to emphasise is that of poverty and social exclusion. The words God, cruci-fied, grace, redemption, saviour, sin, sacrament are interpreted differently depending on the context in which they are spoken and heard; they are spoken and heard in very different ways in an academic lecture hall in Europe than in the slums of a large city in an impoverished country. The perspective of the marginalised and socially excluded is critically important for liberation theology as it insists that Jesus of Nazareth made an option for the poor and that his disciples must do the same if they are to interpret authentically his message for later generations. Only from this perspective can one en-counter anew the liberating power of the gospel and the extra-ordinary responsibility it places on those who take its de-mands seriously. The gospel is all about liberating people from that which oppresses them. According to Segundo, rituals can become terribly oppressive.

Segundo has applied a liberation methodology with great force to Catholic theology in general and to sacramental theo-logy in particular.[37] For him the great questions of our time are posed by hunger, poverty, domination and social exclus-ion. The great danger of ritual activity is that it can completely ignore unjust structures by anaesthetising participants in the ritual act to the realities of their lives, while offering magical access to divine powers. Magic is the great temptation for all participants in ritual acts. Such magic makes people instru-

37. Juan Luis Segundo, *The Liberation of Theology*, New York: Orbis Books 1976; *The Sacraments Today*, Dublin: Gill and Macmillan 1980.

ments rather than subjects of their own history; people go in search of security and special powers which are only accessible through this special rite. Such an approach robs people of their responsibility for themselves and for others. It suggests that there is another way, a magical way, through which one can control the future. Magic lifts one out of the profane world into a sacred sphere wherein one can harness, for one's own benefit, strange powers not normally accessible. The only access to this sacred realm is through particular rites and rituals: through them we become part of a sacred world; without them we are lost in a profane world. Such magical rituals are, according to Segundo, utterly anti-Christian.

Many people find Segundo's critique of the magical traits in traditional rituals too severe. But one can only properly understand his critique when one gives due weight to what he perceives to be two central tenets of Christian belief: '(1) the cultic realm has been relativised and put in the service of liberative human relationships; (2) God's saving grace has been conferred in all its plenitude once and for all.'[38] Jesus' proclamation of the dawning kingdom of God put all ritual acts, including even those of the Jerusalem temple, in service of that kingdom. In other words, through Jesus Christ the sacred has laid hold of and transformed the profane. To be human is already to be part of a sacred realm since God, in Christ, whom Christians believe to be God present in the world, has reached into human history and transformed it into salvation history. The goal of human life in Christ is to liberate human beings for God's future; everything, including all rituals, must now be put in service of this future. As a result, every ritual, if it is to be truly Christian, must raise people's consciousness and become a celebration of their liberative action in history. One could schematise Segundo's argument as follows:

38. J. L. Segundo, *The Sacraments Today*, p. 26.

Scheme (a) represents a magical understanding as it suggests that the people only become sacred through participation in certain ritual acts. In other words, the ritual is more important than the people, as it is the ritual which is holy and opens the door to the sacred sphere; such a conception turns the participants in the ritual into instruments rather than subjects of their own history; instead of awakening them to a renewed sense of community and responsibility, it robs them of their true dignity in making them dependent on and probably very fearful of strange powers and dominations. Rituals which follow this model should be rejected by Christians.

Scheme (b) represents a very brief and accurate outline of Christian history. Christians believe that God in Christ transformed everything human into something radically sacred, making them God's own people who then celebrate and deepen their identity through various rituals. Notice how central the communal dimension is in this scheme of things: rituals do not provide magical access to divine powers but rather God has created a people, a community, in which sacred rites ceaselessly affirm and challenge its true identity. This is what it means to move from magic to prophecy, from abandoning ourselves to strange powers to embracing responsibility for our present and our future. All of this can be summarised in one principle: the people are primordial, the rituals are secondary.

One further emphasis in Segundo's methodology which is important for our reflections here is the critical role he gives

to political consciousness. Throughout history those with political power have attempted to use religious ritual to legitimate their power. One of the great examples of this was in the
eighth century BC in official Yahwism, where the political
upper classes were effectively 'controlling' God for their own
purposes. The prophets Amos and Hosea critiqued this with
such force that their words are as real today, almost three
thousand years later. True religious ritual will always question
the cosy securities of the present political system; false religious ritual effectively becomes part of a civil religion, indis-
tinguishable from all the other aspects of civic life. Religious
rituals are constantly tempted to become part of such a civil
religion, justifying the *status quo* politically, socially and economically. Then there is no bite and no critique of who we are
and no challenge to become more authentic. Ritual must not
seek to encapsulate the incomprehensible God, rather truly
efficacious rituals will open people to the mystery of God.
Magical rites control the divine for some ideological purpose.
Instead of awakening the participants anew to their dignity
and responsibility, these rituals do nothing more than lend
credibility and divine sanction to present structures. As they
become more reified, these rituals lose all sense of the liminal
and *communitas*. For Segundo such rituals have descended
into the realms of an unChristian legitimation of existing
power structures.

One might summarise Segundo's critique of religious ritual
as follows: (i) rituals which are a true celebration of Christian
faith should invite participants to enter more deeply into the
mystery of God while affirming communal identity and challenging social responsibility; (ii) rituals tend to become magical and so enslave people; (iii) Christians must be acutely
aware of the dangers of their rituals becoming part of a civil
religion. It is interesting to apply these principles to the history
of ritual expression in the Irish context. If one takes the exam-

ples of the festival of *Lughnasa* and the pilgrimage to Lough
Derg, the very least one can argue is that those rituals were as
much in tune with Segundo's principles as the newer rites of
the 'devotional revolution' and Anglican proselytism that
sought to displace them. Indeed traditional Irish Catholic ritual expression evolved over centuries as precisely a critique of
civil religion: the rituals and symbols of British rule – the
monarchy, the Westminster parliament, the landlord's house,
the Protestant faith – were put in question by an alternative
ritual structure. This probably helps to explain the consistently
vehement attacks of Protestant writers on traditional Irish religious rituals over several centuries. Turner goes so far as to
claim that the pilgrimage to Lough Derg symbolised Ireland
as the 'martyr nation' and provided ritual access to a radically
counter-cultural interpretation of society and politics.[39]
However, with the establishment of the independent Irish
State after 1921, there was almost complete identification of
church and State rituals. This is precisely the danger that
Segundo warns against; in trying to reform and renew our rituals we will have to eradicate any vestiges of a civil religion because being a disciple will invariably mean being challenged
to live in a counter culture with rituals that go against the
cultural grain. Such rituals today will have to open people to
the liminal, awakening a sense of the numinous and the mysterious, stirring the great powers of wonder and awe, creating
small dynamic communities where people feel wanted and
cared for, whilst affirming and challenging commitment.

(3) A renewed theological imagination

Can we trust the human imagination? Religious iconoclasts have always demanded its purification, but one could
equally well understand the imagination as the wellspring of
God's revelation. It's difficult to believe that a religion with

39. Victor Turner and Edith Turner, *Image and Pilgrimage* ..., p. 136.

belief in the incarnation of the divine as its central doctrine, and the breaking of bread as its core ritual, could be so negative about so many aspects of human expression. The gradual privatisation of Christianity over the past two hundred years is in stark contrast with the life of the primitive Christian churches where the Lord and the Spirit were recognised in the communal rituals of eucharist and baptism. The pious individualism of contemporary Christianity is doubtful territory for retrieving these foundational experiences of what it is to be a disciple. Despite all their attendant dangers of succumbing to fertility rites, the rituals of our forebears were probably better ground for encountering the *communitas* at the heart of Christian experience. If we are to renew and reform our ritual expressions for the times in which we live, we will have to foster a vibrant theological imagination. In doing so we have much to learn from the past.

As we attempt to decipher our past we must be careful not to dismiss the religious experience of our forebears as little more than pre-modern ritualism. Poor and broken people are always iconophile. They reach out for whatever help they can find and will place their trust in any power that might save them. The iconoclasm of the well-fed stomach should at least hesitate in its theological judgments. Hunger stalked the land of Ireland many times in the nineteenth century; most shockingly of all it revisited the people of Connacht thirty years after the Great Hunger in the late 1870s. In 1879 the poor of Connacht were in a wretched state, there was nothing to celebrate around *Lughnasa* time as the potato crop failed for the third year in a row, and on 21 August several people claimed to see a Marian apparition on the gable wall of the church in Knock. Michael Davitt's land war was about to begin and the word 'boycott' would soon enter the English language. Yet again the complex iconography of Irish Catholics was expressing itself.

The religious imagination of Irish Catholics can be understood only in the context of the land that was fought over, the
famine that was endured and the language that was lost.
Land, famine, language – could one think of more potent
forces for forming the imagination? Poets, dramatists, artists
and musicians have stirred the wells of the Irish religious
imagination but surely all believers need to do likewise. We
could do so by re-awakening a sense of the power of our ritual
traditions. Here is one simple example. There are places in
the countryside and places in the soul where the spirit of the
Great Hunger is hauntingly present; we can revisit these
spaces through imaginative ritual. Imagine, for instance, the
significance of a small community gathering to honour an
unmarked mass grave from the 1840s, to admit the pain of
history, to pray for responsible leadership, to hope for justice
and to lay to rest finally those who died such terrible deaths.
It is ritual with its openness to this liminal, *communitas* encounter with the dead which can help us to celebrate and not
simply to study the past.

A vibrant Irish theological imagination must be open to
the various strands of ritual traditions that have formed and
continue to form the complex reality of Irish Catholicism.
The latter is, as was said at the beginning of this chapter, a
traditional religion. It comprises beliefs, practices, rituals and
customs which constitute a living incarnate religion functioning in a very practical way as an interpretative model of
human existence. It brings together in an apparently 'unholy
alliance' the residue of archaic fertility rites, land-based rituals,
orthodox Christian beliefs and a broad notion of the sacramentality of life. This traditional religion is still manifest in
popular religiosity today: pilgrimages to Knock, Lourdes,
Fatima and Medjugorje abound; making the rounds and saying one's prayers at ancient sites like Lough Derg, Croagh
Patrick and lesser known mountains and holy wells is com-

mon; novenas and missions pack churches up and down the country; devotions to Padre Pio, Martin de Porres and Maria Goretti still thrive among some groups; the blessing of throats and the distribution of ashes occasion large gatherings of the community. Nothing could be more elitist, or as vivid an example of cultural exclusivism, than simply dismissing these traditions as a conservative people clinging to a dead past, though this is what scholars in areas as diverse as theology, philosophy, pastoral care and sociology have tended to do.

At the dawn of the third millennium we need to re-awaken our theological imagination so as to mediate the divine in ways that are ever ancient and ever new. But we need criteria to help us establish what rituals can be renewed and suffused with new power, and what rituals are incompatible with Christian belief. The latter must be rejected or simply let die away. We have already pointed towards some of these criteria in the writings of St Paul and Juan Luis Segundo; we will continue this task in chapter six. In the meantime our attention will turn in the next chapter to a retrieval of the key principles of the Catholic sacramental tradition and the conclusions we might draw from these principles for the renewal of religious ritual today.

Traditional Principles
in Catholic Sacramental Theology

Those societies which cannot combine reverence to their symbols with freedom and revision, must ultimately decay either from anarchy, or from the slow atrophy of a life stifled by useless shadows.

A. N. Whitehead

The key elements of the Catholic sacramental tradition can be summarised in seven principles. To ignore these principles is effectively to cut oneself off from the *sensus fidelium* which has emerged in the sacramental practice of Catholics over two millennia. Those who reject these principles have traditionally been characterised as heretical. Although today one would like to avoid the language of heresy, it seems at best arrogant, or at worst deceitful, to ignore the accumulated wisdom of two thousand years of ritual practice. As acknowledged earlier in this book, treasuring the archaic is a dominant motif in revitalising our ritual expression. Yet, as will become clear in our reflections upon these principles, archaic traditions can become fossilised: the Pharisee still occupies the chair of Moses but his words are empty repetitions; the awe-filled claims of baptism are still sounded but they ring hollow in the lives of the faithful; the eucharist is still bread broken for a new world but it lacks newness and vision; couples exchange the words of consent in marriage but the dignity and commitment of those who speak them is neither challenged nor affirmed. The task then of breathing new life into these archaic traditions remains so that the word might have power, baptism might give life, the eucharist might unleash energy for the future, and marriage might prepare the way for the final nuptial banquet. In addressing this task, there is much wisdom to be garnered from the following principles.

(1) Baptism can never be repeated

This principle evolved from one of the most ferocious debates in the history of Christianity. It began with the persecution of Christians by the emperor Diocletian early in the fourth century. This was probably the most violent persecution of the early church and it occurred just a few short years before Constantine's edict of toleration in 313AD which gave Christians the right to practise their faith unhindered. Religious ritual was at the heart of the issue: would Christians offer sacrifice in honour of the deified emperor and the other gods of the empire or would they not? Many, particularly in North Africa, refused to do so; like the soldier Marcellus they would only subject themselves to one *sacramentum* – that of Christ. The Latin word *sacramentum* was the term used to describe the oath made by a soldier upon entry to a legion of the Roman army. Early Christians used this term to describe the commitment demanded by baptism. During the Diocletian persecution such commitment meant that large numbers of believers were martyred. But many other Christians apostasised. They betrayed their faith in the face of violent persecution. When the terrible violence came to an end most of these people returned to the fold of the church. The great question was should they be accepted back and under what conditions? A bishop called Donatus in North Africa argued vociferously that such people must be re-baptised as they had nullified their earlier baptism through betraying the faith. Similarly, the sacraments administered by priests who had been less than martyr-like in their defence of the faith were useless. In other words, for Donatus and Donatism, the heresy that took its name from him, the church was the church of the élite. It was the church of the pure whose members proved their purity and sinlessness by their willingness to endure martyrdom. Those who proved themselves less than perfectly holy were not truly baptised Christians at all.

Donatism tore the North African church apart throughout the fourth century. When Augustine of Hippo (354-430) appeared on the ecclesial scene towards the end of that century, he perceived Donatism to be one of the greatest threats to the life of the church. In order to appreciate Augustine's condemnation of the Donatists it is necessary to consider his own experience of conversion. After leading a carefree life he attempted to reform himself through strenuous efforts and strict intentions. But these great expectations ended in abject failure. Then Augustine encountered Christ and his life changed. He believed his conversion and baptism to be pure gift, utterly unmerited on his part, a demonstration of what divine power could achieve in the most unlikely of persons. Therefore, he was ill at ease with any theological outlook which suggested that the human person could merit salvation. For Augustine, the church was all about sinners who were given the free gift of grace in baptism, whereas for the Donatists, the church was the community of the baptised called to live a life of perfect holiness. Those who failed to do so were not really baptised at all. In time Augustine's position won out and the church came to see baptism as God's work – gracious, efficacious and irrepeatable. Even if one fails to live up to the demands of one's baptism one cannot destroy God's gift. Even if one renounces one's baptism one can never nullify God's offer of salvation. The Christian might be unfaithful, God is always faithful.

Donatism had disappeared by the end of the sixth century, its very last vestiges swept away by Islamic invasion. But the idea that the church is only for the deeply committed, and that the less than full-blooded should be excluded, has continued to exist in different forms throughout history. The most famous example of this was found amongst anabaptists – which literally means the 'rebaptisers' – who vehemently rejected infant baptism and demanded that adults be rebaptised in what they called 'believer's baptism'. This implied that the baptism of infants was effectively the baptism of unbelievers. All mainstream churches have rejected this position in their embrace of baptism as the free gift of God's Spirit which immerses us in the paschal mystery of Christ, creates the fellowship of believers, washes away sin and opens the way to a new future. This wondrous gift can never be repeated since it will never be revoked.

(2) We are saved by God's free gift of grace

Just when Augustine had finished his polemics against the Donatists, an even more serious theological trend emerged in Rome itself. Pelagius, a priest from a Celtic background, came to Rome around the same time as Augustine. He appears to have come from a strict monastic setting and was scandalised with the lax morals and uninspiring ecclesial life of the indigenous Roman church. The rigours associated with entry into the Christian community were effectively being abandoned in the post-Constantinian church which was overwhelmed by new converts. Pelagius was not impressed by what he saw in Rome. People were entering the waters of baptism without proper formation and, even worse, many of those who had passed through the waters of baptism were not living up to the moral standards demanded of Christians. As a result, Pelagius began to call into question the real efficacy of baptism. How could one be baptised and still continue to live the old life of sin? Surely such a baptism is not truly salvific?

Thoughts such as these formed the theological trend known to later generations as Pelagianism. At their extreme, Pelagians argued that Christianity is all about human freedom, the challenge to grow in perfection by always choosing the good. In making these moral choices Christ is a good example and Adam is a bad example. Baptism is the challenge to perfection; the church is the community of those who attempt to live perfectly holy lives. Not surprisingly, Pelagius probably believed that the best context for forming such good Christian habits was the strict monastery. Certainly the lack lustre moral ambience of the declining city of Rome at the close of the fourth century (where seemingly anyone and everyone could be called a Christian) was, for Pelagius, the antithesis of Christian living. Again, as in the case of Donatism, Augustine was roused into a powerful response.

As far as Augustine was concerned, Pelagius completely misinterpreted the nature of Christianity. The Pelagians seemed to suggest that salvation is as much our doing as it is God's work in that they questioned the efficacy of baptism for those who failed to live up to the strict moral demands of Christian living. But Augustine argued that salvation is purely God's free gift and is given to us in baptism. The baptised are called to live a Christian life in response to the great gift they have received, but the gift is God's work and without it they are nothing at all. Left to their own devices, Augustine insists, humans are going nowhere. This is why he is so negative about the fate of the unbaptised and why he even went so far as to say that unbaptised infants are lost. This extraordinarily extreme position evolved from his total mistrust of human endeavour. We cannot lift ourselves out of the miry pit in which we find ourselves; God must reach down to save us. The Pelagians believed that what we had to do was to find the ladder and pull ourselves out of the pit slowly but surely. Augustine saw Adam, not as a bad example, but as the one who has plunged all humanity into sin; Christ is not only a good example but the saviour and redeemer of all people. Baptism is therefore our immersion into the power of Christ and the church is a community of sinners on the way to salvation.

For our purposes, it's important to note why the Augustinian position became the benchmark for orthodoxy. Augustine emphasised that it is God who takes the initiative. Christian living can only be understood as a response to this divine gift. Furthermore, he insisted that Christ is the key to this gift and that one must be baptised in Christ if one is to be saved. This baptismal gift is freely available to all. Sadly for someone who was so consumed by the gratuity of God's gift in Christ, Augustine never accepted the universality of this gift so he could never understand how those who were not baptised might be saved. The tragic legacy of this theological perspective is only too well known; children who died without baptism were, according to Augustine, lost forever and according to later theological opinion they were consigned to limbo. One way or the other, fear and guilt were sown in the minds and hearts of sincere believers and baptism became equated in the popular mind with saving babies from eternal damnation rather than celebrating the wondrous divine gift of life and rebirth in Christ. Somehow I feel that Augustine himself would be deeply saddened by this legacy, for there can be no doubt but that the main aim in his debates with the Donatists and the Pelagians was to awaken all people to God's free gift of grace in Christ. This fundamental principle would inform further developments in sacramental theology in later centuries.

(3) There are seven sacraments

It took the church over a millennium to finally decide on the number of sacraments. Only in the twelfth century was the number seven finally accepted. The Second Council of

Lyons[1] in 1274 clearly identifies the seven sacraments as baptism, confirmation, eucharist, penance, extreme unction, orders and marriage. These seven have been accepted by the Catholic Church ever since. While the next four principles will analyse what the term 'sacrament' actually means in the Catholic Church, the focus for now is on the number of sacraments.

Why seven? Has it anything to do with the seven days of creation in Genesis – the old creation emerged in seven days and the new creation is already encountered but not yet complete in the seven sacraments? Or maybe it is linked to the seven weeks between Easter Day and Pentecost Day, suggesting that we encounter the risen Christ in these seven Spirit-filled sacramental rituals? Or is it the deep symbolism of the number seven itself constituted as it is by the addition of the numbers three and four; in primitive societies three symbolised time, e.g. the three phases of the moon, while four often symbolised space, e.g. north, south, east and west or the four corners of the earth; adding three and four brings space and time together in the mysterious number seven, maybe indicating that in these seven rituals we have a foretaste of the eschatological fulfilment beyond the limitations of time and space? We do not really know the answer to these questions; maybe there is some truth in all of the suggestions above. But what we do know for sure is that throughout history theologians have seriously disagreed on the number of sacramental rituals at the core of Christian belief – some believed that there were as many as twelve or thirteen whilst others were absolutely certain that there were only two.

Before reading any further, ask yourself what other sacraments could there be. Keep in mind the basic theological principle that sacraments must be linked to Jesus' own min-

1. The original text can be found in Denzinger-Schonmetzer (DS), op. cit. 860. There is an English translation in Neuner and Dupuis (ND), op. cit. 28.

istry and must give us a share in divine life. In the early Middle Ages, arguments were made for the sacramental status of rituals like the washing of feet, the blessing of corpses, the taking of religious vows, going on pilgrimage and the distribution of ashes on Ash Wednesday. Furthermore, a case could be made for the inclusion of the public proclamation of the scriptures, funeral rites outside of Mass and various types of prayer gatherings. Given these other possibilities, it is not so surprising that it took a millennium to finally decide that particular significance attaches to the seven rituals called sacraments, notwithstanding the fact that other rituals and symbols are also important in Christian belief. It is interesting to note that both the Eastern Orthodox Churches and the Catholic Church came to much the same conclusions concerning the seven sacraments. However, the Protestant Churches that evolved from the Reformation in the sixteenth century had a very different opinion.

Protestantism in general recognises just two sacraments – baptism and eucharist – because these are the only two with expressed scriptural warrant. This argument revolves around the principle of Christ's institution of the sacraments which we will analyse below. Overall one should notice the different theological spirit that has imbued the Reformed Churches with their critique of the very broad use of symbol and ritual in the Catholic Church and the Orthodox Churches. Yet once more, this is the clash of the iconoclast with the iconophile, a theological struggle which echoes throughout history. As we look to the future, it is the argument of this book that, notwithstanding the emphasis of the Catholic Church on the seven sacraments, we will need to unleash our ritual creativity anew in the third millennium.

(4) Three of the sacraments give a special character
The sacraments of baptism, confirmation and orders can-

not be repeated because they give a special character. The
Council of Florence (1439) taught that:

> Among these sacraments (the seven) there are three, bap-
> tism, confirmation and orders, which imprint on the soul
> an indelible character, that is a certain spiritual sign distin-
> guishing the recipient from others. Hence, these are not
> repeated for the same person. The other four, however, do
> not imprint a character and may be repeated.[2]

This issue brings us back to the very origins of sacramental
theology. The Greek word 'character' referred to an indelible
mark like the inscription of a head on a coin or an irremov-
able seal burnt into the flesh of an animal or a human being
so that they were marked for life with this new identity. Early
Christians made use of this word in their understanding of
baptism as they believed that the neophyte, the one newly
born through the waters of baptism, was sealed with a new
identity, indelibly marked for a new way of living. Today
when we speak of a person's character we mean the truth of
who the person really is, that which goes far deeper than appearances and touches the soul of the person's life. This is precisely what early Christians meant by the word 'character'. As
a result of his debates with the Donatists, Augustine taught
that in baptism and orders one receives a 'character', akin to a
seal burnt into one's flesh, which marks a person indelibly and
means that these rites cannot be repeated. This was the theological origin of phrases like 'once a priest, always a priest'; as
true as this is, one should remember that it is theologically
just as valid and important to say 'once baptised, always baptised'. Many centuries later, Thomas Aquinas further developed this thinking when he said that three sacraments onto-
logically change the recipient; through participation in these
religious rituals one is really changed into a new reality different from what one was before. By 'ontological change'

2. DS 1313; ND 1308.

Aquinas meant more than a psychological or sociological adaptation to a new situation; rather as a result of the sacramental ritual, be it baptism, confirmation or orders, something radically new was created in the person.

It is interesting to note a link here with the work of contemporary cultural anthropologists like Victor Turner. Turner's analysis of some primitive rituals, especially key rites of passage, leads one to much the same conclusions as the traditional claims concerning sacramental character. Through the ritual process the participants are radically changed, one could almost say indelibly marked, in a way that sets them apart from others, and then they return or reaggregate with a new identity. Because one is bestowed with a new identity through the ritual, one can only participate in it once. The echoes of medieval sacramental theology can certainly be heard in this twentieth-century anthropological study of ritual practices. Perhaps this goes to show that earlier Christian thought was more in tune with the rhythms of human life than modern thinkers would care to admit.

One should remember that Christianity fully accepts the ancient Jewish belief that humans are made in God's image *(eikon)* and likeness; in the original creation they are God's icon and in the new creation they are sealed with a new identity, bearing the imprint of a new character. The word 'Christ' means 'the anointed one' and in the sacraments of baptism, confirmation and orders Christians are anointed with the same Spirit with which Jesus was anointed in the Jordan. The anointings, which are a central element in these three sacraments, suggest that the overwhelming dignity of the original creation in God's image is transfigured as Christians become God's own anointed. The first creation bestows dignity beyond measure and the new creation gives an identity which words cannot express but which is encountered and celebrated in symbol and ritual. How to retrieve and re-articulate this ancient Christian belief is one of the great pastoral challenges facing the church today. The renewal of baptism, confirmation and orders must be linked in such a way that the anointed priestly character of those who celebrate these rituals is manifested and celebrated. We should benefit from the work of authors like Turner in understanding just how inseparable are the ritual and the new identity which the ritual initiates.

(5) The seven sacraments were instituted by Christ

The claim that the seven key rites of the Catholic Church were instituted by Christ is one of the most debated of all claims in the history of sacramental theology. It became one of the central issues in the Protestant Reformation of the sixteenth century. Protestant theology developed a strong suspicion concerning the biblical foundations of several sacraments. Eventually, Protestant thinkers in the main affirmed that there were only two rites with sufficient scriptural attestation to warrant the title 'sacrament'. These two were, of course, baptism and eucharist. In the various texts of the Christian scriptures there are clear indications in one form or another of the significance of these two rituals in the life of the early Christian communities. These themes are echoed in the writings of the fathers of the church; indeed expressing the full riches of these rites was one of the main emphases in patristic theology. From a Protestant perspective, the other five sacraments lacked explicit scriptural warrant; to insist that Christ instituted these rites as sacraments was to go much further than the scriptural evidence allowed.

In reaction to the criticisms of the Reformers, the Council of Trent (1545-1562) stoutly re-affirmed the doctrine of the Catholic Church that the seven sacraments were instituted by Christ.[3] The critical question then is what does 'instituted' mean? On the basis of modern historical scholarship we can

3. DS 1601; ND 1311.

say for certain what institution does not mean: it does not mean that the various elements that constitute the seven sacramental rites that we have today all go back to an explicit command of Jesus. We now know that many structural elements in the rituals have changed over the centuries; furthermore, it is theologically unnecessary to link every aspect of the seven rituals we have today to some direct command found on Jesus' lips in the gospels. What is theologically necessary, in the light of the teaching of the Council of Trent, is to demonstrate that the later sevenfold expression of sacramental life is clearly rooted in the ministry of Jesus. In other words, 'institution' demands that the meaning behind these rituals – the forgiveness of sin, the gift of the Holy Spirit, the enduring presence of Christ, the call for reconciliation, the healing of the sick, the demand for radical commitment in human relationships, the setting apart of some disciples for special ministry – must be found in Jesus' own ministry.[4] Surely it is clear that one can indeed find these realities in the ministry of Jesus and this is the minimum that is required in order to say that Christ instituted the sevenfold sacramental structure. Clearly the apostolic and patristic church adapted these meanings for different contexts and the various rituals associated with them evolved over several centuries. Some of these rituals, notably baptism and eucharist, are already present in the scriptural accounts while others, like confirmation and orders, owe more to the faith and theological reflection of the first few centuries of Christian belief. Given this historical evolution and the Catholic teaching that the seven rites were instituted by Christ, can the later church change these rituals?

The answer to this question has to be 'yes' and 'no'. Yes the church can adapt its core rituals to new situations, adding elements which unblock the wellsprings of faith in the hearts

4. See Liam G. Walsh, *The Sacraments of Initiation*, London: Geoffrey Chapman 1988, pp. 58-59.

and minds of believers and seeking to focus participants on what really matters by shedding some later accretions.[5] However, the church cannot change the meaning behind the ritual or reject the interpretation of these meanings in the life of the apostolic and early patristic church. Why does the early church have this much significance? The greatest modern writer on the sacraments is Edward Schillebeeckx. He argued strenuously that we should not follow medieval theology in attempting to define the moment that Jesus instituted each of the seven sacraments; rather we should understand these rites as emerging from the death and resurrection of Jesus.[6] What was primarily instituted as a result of the life, death and resurrection of Jesus was a community of believers. The seven sacraments must be understood in the context of the communal life and developing beliefs of the early Christians. Remember that these early communities in cities like Jerusalem and Antioch were celebrating their faith in rituals long before any of the early Christian writings emerged. From the beginning they were baptising people and coming together for the breaking of bread; in Palestine they continued to participate in the synagogues and in Jerusalem they still took part in the temple cult.

But the death and resurrection of Jesus had instituted or sowed the seeds of a new community. From the very outset this community remembered and encountered the Lord through ritual; these rituals were a critical element in its self-understanding, maybe even the most important element of all. As time went on these new communities drifted away or were excluded from Jewish traditions, and so they naturally began to express the meaning of their own faith in evolving

5. Second Vatican Council, *Sacrosanctum Concilium*: The Constitution on the Sacred Liturgy, 62.
6. Edward Schillebeeckx, *Christ the Sacrament of Encounter With God*, London: Sheed and Ward 1963, pp. 137-163.

rituals. In this new liturgical context, questions arose such as: who will lead this community? who should preside at the gatherings for the breaking of the bread? what does marriage mean in the light of our new faith? what do we do about someone who sins seriously having been baptised? what did Jesus mean by the healing of the sick? Reflecting on these and similar questions, the church finally settled on seven rites as particularly important. In order to appreciate the significance of the principle that Christ instituted the seven sacraments, one must then draw together the ministry of Jesus, the mystery of his death and resurrection, the community that emerged as a result of belief in the resurrection, and the experience of the presence of the Holy Spirit in that community.

(6) The sacraments are effective ex opere operato

This is one of the most controversial of all the claims made about the seven Catholic sacraments; simultaneously it is one of the most important. The principle sounds complicated but in fact it is rather simple. The claim is that the sacraments are effective 'by the work worked' or, in more comprehensible English, 'by the performance of the rite'. This means that if the rite is properly performed then that which the rite signifies actually happens; so one begins to speak of the sacraments as causing that which they signify, as efficacious signs of grace (signum efficax) and as outward signs which effect that which they signify. So in baptism one is not just pouring water but washing in a much deeper sense and being immersed in the mystery of Christ and the church; in the eucharist one partakes not just of bread and wine but of the body and blood of Christ; in marriage one is not just talking about human love but actually getting married; in anointing of the sick one is not just smeared with oil but exposed to the healing ministry of Christ. This then is what it means to say that the sacraments are effective ex opere operato: through the proper performance of the rite that which is symbolised actually occurs in that having passed through the ritual I am baptised, confirmed, married, ordained, reconciled, anointed or I have partaken of the body and blood of Christ. This is precisely the Catholic understanding of the seven sacraments.

Clearly this principle is making very strong claims about the nature of these rituals. It does so on the basis of the previous principle – that Christ instituted these rituals as sacraments. As a result, one can have faith that these rituals are effective *ex opere operato;* if Christ is not active in the sacraments then they are the most empty of rituals. Because Christ is active in the sacraments then we can speak of the seven rites as bestowing grace, as causing that which they signify, i.e. as expressing and attaining in human life (through grace) a divine reality (the giving of the Holy Spirit, the forgiveness of sin, etc.). Such awe-inspiring claims were unfortunately subject to abuse and misinterpretation.

The most dangerous abuses and misinterpretations were focussed on the power of the ordained minister. Surely, many argued, this principle vests the priest with power over the divine; all he has to do is go through the rubrics of the ritual and then, magically, God's grace is given. In medieval times there certainly were many abuses on the part of priests: some were almost biblically illiterate while sacramentally very active. At times there were terrible contradictions between the lifestyle of the priest and the sacramental rites that he administered and, most unseemly of all, there crept into Catholic practice a terrible minimalism, the key issue being what was the minimum that the priest and participants had to do for the sacrament to be effective *ex opere operato*. This minimalism leads even today to the most questionable pastoral practices such as an overwhelming emphasis on the priest in the sacramental gathering to the near exclusion of all others, utterly impoverished celebrations which are rushed through because they are valid anyway, very poor preparation and, most objectionably of all, the wandering cleric who will perform any sacrament any place any time. Such practices undermine the true meaning of this principle and recall once again the debates of the sixteenth century.

Protestant Reformers objected strenuously against what they perceived as the very worst expressions of priestly magic and it was in this polemical atmosphere that some began to speak of the actions of the priest during Mass as hocus-pocus. The Council of Trent staunchly defended this principle in the face of the critique of the Reformers.[7] In doing so it was affirming important aspects of Catholic tradition; for the sacrament to be valid the minister must intend to do that which the church does in the sacrament[8] and, with regard to participants, they must not place any obstacle *(obex)* in the way of the sacrament.[9] These are two significant points: notice the importance of the intention of the minister; the priest must intend to baptise, to bestow God's forgiveness, to call the Holy Spirit upon the bread and wine and to anoint; the bishop must intend to invoke the Holy Spirit and to ordain; the couple in marriage must intend to marry each other; such is the minimum requirement of the minister if the sacramental rite is to be valid. But the minister's lifestyle, opinions, moral standing and even his or her lack of faith do not invalidate the sacrament once the minister intends to do that which the church does. A few examples will demonstrate the consequences of this: a bishop may have a personal crisis of faith in God but the sacramental rites that he ministers are still valid provided he intends to do that which the church does even if he finds it difficult or impossible to believe; the lifestyle of a priest might be in clear contradiction of gospel values but he can still be a

7. DS 1608; ND 1318.
8. DS 1611; ND 1321.
9. DS 1606; ND 1316.

minister of valid sacraments; a woman and man might have
little idea of the personal, emotional and financial implications of marriage on their wedding day but they are validly
married provided they intend to marry each other; and
maybe most importantly today one should highlight the example of moral failure – a priest who is guilty of murder or
sexual abuse or theft can still validly celebrate the sacramental
rites provided he intends to do that which the church does in
the particular ritual. The other issue which must be addressed
in terms of the validity of the sacraments is that of obstacles
which, when present, invalidate a sacrament that appears to
be valid. The obvious examples are: baptism – having been
previously baptised; confirmation – not having been baptised; eucharist – the celebrant is not ordained; marriage – inability to give valid consent due to previous marriage, ordination, age, insanity, impotence, psychological immaturity or
extreme pressure. When such obstacles are present the particular sacramental rite, notwithstanding all appearances to the
contrary, is invalid; the grace of Christ is not bestowed. But
whenever a minister intends to do that which the church does
and there is no obstacle present, then the sacrament is valid
and effective by the very performance of the rite, *ex opere operato*.

The problem with maxims such as *ex opere operato*, 'intending to do what the church does' and 'no obstacles' is that
they invariably get interpreted in a minimalist manner. Thus
the question becomes: what is the minimum necessary for the
sacrament to be valid? This mindset can give rise to the most
grotesque pastoral practices such as 'quick Masses', private
sacraments and an interaction with symbol that borders on
the ridiculous in its parsimonious use of bread, wine, water
and oil, as if these basics of human life were in dire short sup-
ply. At different times in the history of the church such minimalism got completely out of hand; many believe that it was

the most serious cause of the Protestant Reformation. This is a tragic irony, for the most christological of the principles that we are analysing is that the sacraments are effective by the very performance of the rite, and the Reformation was nothing if not a christological critique of current church practices. Today we need to extricate ourselves from any minimalist or magical interpretations of *ex opere operato*. The principle refers to the power of Christ, not the power of the priest. In Christ God entered human history and has begun to transform it from within. Through the death and resurrection of Christ ancient symbols and rituals are vested with new significance and God's own life is encountered in the waters of baptism, the gift of the Holy Spirit, the forgiveness of sin, the healing of the sick, the intimate committed love of spouses, the ministry of the ordained and in the food and drink of the eucharist. To make these claims is not to suggest that priests are magicians but that God in Christ has begun to transform all human life and to raise it to share in the divine. The lifelong task of the priest is to conform his life to that of Christ so that there is no contradiction between his personal and ministerial roles, but given our frail humanity such contradictions are bound to ensue; the teaching of the church is that the power of Christ can overcome even these contradictions.

There are two other perspectives on the meaning of *ex opere operato* which are especially interesting. Earlier we saw a possible link between the work of Victor Turner and the theology of sacramental character; similarly one can draw parallels between the work of cultural anthropologists and the theological maxim – *ex opere operato*. In their analysis of rites of passage, both Van Gennep and Turner believed that something happened as a result of the performance of the rite that would not otherwise occur; in other words, the very performance of the rite causes a new reality. This is exactly what traditional Catholic theology meant by the term *ex opere operato,* the difference between the theological and the anthropological approaches being that the former believes that the power of Christ is active in the ritual. But there is another insight that we can draw from traditional theology that is even more pertinent for renewing religious ritual today. It is Catholic doctrine that there are seven sacraments and that these seven rites are effective *ex opere operato* because Christ is present and active in them. But one need not conclude from this that *only* the seven sacraments are effective *ex opere operato*. The teaching of the church is not that only seven rituals are effective but that one can be certain as regards the efficacy of these seven rites. Therefore the possibility remains open that many other rituals might be powerfully effective, not alone in an anthropological sense, but also in renewing and deepening Christian identity. The church will not and should not change the number of sacraments, but its very belief in the power of certain rituals *ex opere operato* surely demands an openness to a broad sense of ritual, not least to emerging forms of ritual creativity today which could make an important contribution to the sacramental renewal of the church.

(7) The sacraments are effective ex opere operantis

To say that the sacraments are effective *ex opere operantis* means that they are effective in terms of the way that the 'rite is received'. Thus the manner in which one approaches a particular sacramental celebration determines how effective that sacrament will be in one's life. A disposition characterised by openness to God's word, faith in Christ's presence, hope in God's promise and love of God's people, will undoubtedly make the sacrament more effective in the life of the particular individual believer. If the previous principle can be described as objective, then this one is subjective; traditionally this is spoken of as the difference between the validity and fruitfulness of a sacramental rite. The implication of the previous principle is that a sacrament is objectively effective whether any particular individual or group of people actually believe in the claims being made for the ritual. The child is baptised whether those present fully grasp what is occurring or not; Christ is present in the eucharistic bread and wine whether I believe it or not; free consent in marriage creates an indissoluble union whether the couple fully appreciate this or not; sin is forgiven in the sacrament of reconciliation whether I can really accept this or not. The implication of this principle is that, though a sacrament might be objectively valid, it can be subjectively unfruitful in the life of a particular individual; a baby is baptised in order to please the grandparents; a youngster is confirmed but is not raised in the practice of the faith; parents insist on their child being admitted to first communion even though they have no attachment to the eucharistic community; a couple get married in church because culturally it is the more acceptable thing to do; the examples are numerous but the implication is the same – the sacramental rite is indeed valid *ex opere operato* but might well be unfruitful *ex opere operantis*. Of course it is difficult to judge how effective a sacrament might be in a person's life, but it seems reasonable to conclude that the fruitfulness of a sacrament is dependent on the disposition of the participant.

Ideally sacraments should be both valid and fruitful; a validly celebrated sacrament will slowly but surely bear fruit in the lives of those who participate in the rite in good faith. A baby is baptised but it takes a lifetime to begin to appreciate the meaning of this ritual bathing. A parishioner goes to Mass every Sunday and partakes of the body of Christ but the awareness only dawns gradually of the social and communal demands that this ritual meal makes. An individual attends the sacrament of reconciliation once a year but the questions raised by the call to reconciliation echo ever more deeply in the depths of one's life. Someone who is seriously ill is anointed but the healing that opens the door towards God's future might bear little fruit before the person dies. Young adults are married or ordained but throughout their lives they encounter over and over again the implications of these long since past rituals. This is what the church means by saying that the sacraments are effective *ex opere operantis,* that the manner in which we receive the sacraments, both on the occasion of the actual celebration and in our later lives, determines the fruitfulness of the sacrament.

Clearly this principle emphasises the importance of faith in the reception of the sacraments. This is precisely the emphasis that the Reformers of the sixteenth century believed was lacking in Catholic sacramental practice. Thus the two traditions separated, not least on the interpretation of the meaning of the sacraments. For many Protestants, Catholic practice was indeed hocus pocus; the demands on one's faith were minimal whilst the sacrament was still effective *ex opere operato.* In rejecting the latter as having more in common with magic than with Christian doctrine, the newly emerging Reformed Churches focussed their attention on faith in God's word and on the two sacraments of the New Testament – baptism and eucharist. Without personal faith the words of scripture were empty repetitions and the sacraments were magical ritualism. So it was that in practice Protestants seldom celebrated the sacraments and Sunday worship was characterised by readings from the bible, hymn singing and sermonising. In contrast, the Catholic Church in hostility to the Reformers brought renewed vigour to sacramental life as the key source of grace. So it was that in practice Catholics seldom read the scriptures but attended the sacraments regularly, though in a very passive manner as the priest was the key figure. As the churches diverged more and more, the Protestant emphasis was on faith and word while Catholics emphasised grace and sacrament. This led to the unhappy outcome that

Protestants had little or no experience of the sacramental life and little love for symbol or ritual, while Catholics were often ignorant of the scriptures and passive observers at Sunday Mass.

The modern ecumenical movement has addressed these issues, leading to a new sacramental sensibility among Protestants and an explosion in interest in the scriptures amongst Catholics. The Second Vatican Council promoted a vision of pastoral renewal centred on word and sacrament; immersing believers in the word of God would lead to a renewed faith expressed in active participation in the sacramental rituals. But more than thirty years after the close of the Council, an important question remains: what faith is required for the sacraments? Take the simplest example: two parents who have not been married in church bring their child for baptism; it is clear to all that the child will not be raised in the practice of the faith and that the main reason the parents are having their child baptised is to avoid family tensions. Should this child be baptised? The answer to this question is not simple. Some will argue (on the basis of *ex opere operato*) that the grace of the sacrament should not be denied to anyone; others will say (on the basis of *ex opere operantis*) that explicit faith is necessary for the sacraments and this faith must be expressed by practising the sacraments. This is the sort of dilemma posed when one tries to give due weight to the two principles that we have been analysing; traditionally Catholics placed more significance on *ex opere operato* than *ex opere operantis;* today many believers think that we need to review the balance between these two principles.

Conclusion

These seven principles bring together the different strands of the Catholic sacramental tradition. Although most of them were formulated in times of conflict they still give us some insight into the nature of our sacramental rituals. Having drawn from the riches and controversies of tradition in our efforts to develop a deeper awareness of sacramental living, we will turn in the next chapter to modern theology.

Modern Trends
in Sacramental Theology

Out of God's infinite glory, may God give you the power through the Spirit for your hidden self to grow strong, so that Christ may live in your hearts through faith, and then, planted in love and built on love, you will with all the saints have strength to grasp the breadth and the length, the height and the depth; until, knowing the love of Christ, which is beyond all knowledge, you are filled with the utter fulness of God. Glory be to God whose power, working in us, can do infinitely more than we can ask or imagine; glory be to God from generation to generation in the church and in Christ Jesus for ever and ever. Amen.

St Paul, Ephesians 3:16-21

The sacramental understanding of the church has been broadened and deepened throughout this century. This chapter is divided into three sections. Firstly, we will analyse the meaning of the claim that Jesus is the sacrament of encounter with God; secondly, our attention will focus on the church as the universal sacrament of salvation, and thirdly, the significance of the existence of two rites of initiation in the Catholic Church will be probed. Various pointers will emerge that could be of benefit in renewing the sacramental life of the church.

Jesus is the sacrament of encounter with God

The varied perspectives of Catholic sacramental thought that have been analysed in the previous chapter evolved over many centuries but were all firmly established by the time of the Council of Trent (1545-62). Twentieth-century sacramental theology has been characterised by a return to the scriptural and patristic (early church) sources. In doing so, it mirrors the drift of all contemporary Catholic theology. This theological renaissance revolved around one issue in particular – the re-discovery of the centrality of the death and resurrection of Christ in Christian belief. Theologians came to see that the church and its rituals only made sense when rooted in the mystery of Christ's death and resurrection. Slowly but surely it emerged that the earliest Christian communities were formed as a result of faith in the resurrection and that this faith was expressed and nourished through the rituals of bap-tism and the 'breaking of bread'. As a result, theologians began to speak of Jesus as the 'primordial', 'foundational' or 'original' sacrament. Various adjectives were used but all with the same intention – to make clear that one was not speaking of Jesus as an eighth sacrament somewhat akin to the other seven but that the life, death and resurrection of Jesus were the foundation or origin of the seven sacraments.

Modern biblical scholarship has established that the texts of the New Testament are not of a journalistic genre intended to be read in much the same way as reportage in a newspaper, but that they are documents of the believing community in-tended to be read in the light of faith. And what is this faith? It is the conviction that Jesus of Nazareth lived and died as a human being, that death could not hold him and that God raised him into the divine reality from which he had originally come. St Paul speaks of this as God's mystery, the plan that God had made in Christ from the beginning (see Eph 1:9). This mystery was unfolded or revealed in Jesus Christ.[1] In trying to articulate such wondrous claims it is always difficult to determine what words one should use. Paul wrote in Greek

---

1. See Second Vatican Council, *Dei Verbum:* Dogmatic Constitution on Divine Revelation, no. 2.

and he used the word *musterion* which is rendered in English as mystery but, interestingly, when the Greek New Testament was translated into Latin by St Jerome in the fourth century, he used the word *sacramentum* to translate *musterion*.[2] Thus it was that Jerome was speaking of the whole plan of salvation as the 'sacrament' of Christ. And it is this sacrament of Christ which is revealed in Jesus' death and resurrection and that finally gives birth to the community of early believers, along with its rituals which would in time be spoken of as sacraments. These various discoveries during the course of this century have led to a renewed christological dimension in sacramental theology. But it was the work of Edward Schillebeeckx which truly brought the person of Christ into focus in our sacramental understanding.

Schillebeeckx's book, *Christ the Sacrament of the Encounter with God*,[3] is one of the most important works in twentieth-century Catholic theology. In it he was attempting to retrieve the sacraments from the clutches of an all too privatised piety and an overly mechanistic model of pastoral practice. Schillebeeckx was influenced by the contemporary phenomenological and existential philosophies of personal encounter. Ever since Descartes, philosophy had been preoccupied with our knowledge of the objective world to the near exclusion of questions of a more personal nature. In the first decades of this century, however, developments in phenomenology and psychology focussed renewed attention on the human person. As the person was treated more as a subject rather than an object, the life experiences of the subject became accepted sources for philosophical reflection. Thus it was that birth and death, relationships and growth, contingency and fear,

---

2. This Latin translation of the bible is known as the Vulgate.
3. Edward Schillebeeckx, *Christ the Sacrament of the Encounter with God*, New York: Sheed and Ward 1963.

love and heartbreak, were acknowledged as the very heartbeat
of human reality. These new emphases had a major influence
on theologians like Schillebeeckx who were convinced that
theology had lost the capacity to truly speak to the human
spirit. He set about changing this with regard to the theology
of the sacraments.

For Schillebeeckx, the all important word is 'encounter';
the sacraments are not objective things that we receive but encounters in which we participate. They mirror the other important encounters in our lives, the relationships and events
which make us who we are. All of these encounters are bodily;
we are not disembodied spirits living in a heavenly world but
true flesh and blood struggling to make the world human.
But our very bodiliness has been transformed through the encounter between humanity and divinity that occurred in the
life of Jesus of Nazareth, the encounter that we traditionally
term the incarnation. The main thing to be said about the incarnation is that it's hard to believe what it claims. The words
roll off our lips very easily – 'the Word was made flesh and lived
amongst us' or 'Jesus was fully human and fully divine' – but it's
quite another matter to really believe these claims and even
more difficult to live our lives as a response to this good news.

Just look at what the word incarnation means; it comes
from the Latin *incarnatus* which means 'made flesh'. The doctrine of the incarnation asks us to believe that God became
one of us, not just like us but fully a part of everything that
makes us human. In other words, to say that Jesus was God
incarnate is to say that, through Jesus, God has become intimately intertwined with the womb and childbirth, childhood
and growing up, joy and loneliness, happiness and sadness,
laughter and tears, old age and the tomb. These fundamental
human experiences are no longer just human but have become a part of the divine. In the life of Jesus, God has become
one with us so that we might become one with God. In other

words, God shares in human life so that we can become sharers in divine life.[4]

The doctrine of the church says that God was fully present in Jesus' humanity; that in the tender presence of Jesus one encountered the divine; Jesus' tears reveal the broken heart of God; Jesus' laughter echoes the divine joy at the wonder of the universe; Jesus' anger is a stirring of divine justice in the midst of the most terrible human injustice and oppression. The life of this poor peasant two thousand years ago was an opening onto the very life of God. When we want to know what God says we must listen to God's Word and that Word is Jesus of Nazareth. One needs to be careful not to romanticise what this means. Jesus lived the most ordinary of human lives: he was born to a poor couple who probably moved to Galilee so that Joseph as a carpenter could get work on the building sites of the new city of Sepphoris; he grew up in an economically backward village; he probably worked as a carpenter; the unjust execution of his cousin John stirred him to go and preach God's mercy and justice. For a couple of years he travelled as a rabbi around the little known villages of Capernaum, Bethsaida, Cana and Naim, preaching that God's reign was dawning in the forgiveness of sinners, in the healing of the sick, in giving new sight to the blind and in binding up the wounds of the broken-hearted.

It was in the very ordinariness of Jesus' life that God spoke the most profound word ever spoken. If we are to hear that word and express it to others we will have to plumb the depths of our own humanity, for it was in the hope and the heartbreak, the plenitude and the poverty, the tenderness and the tragedy, the wonder and the worry of human experience, that Jesus revealed the very depths of God. After Jesus human life is no longer just human; it becomes a vessel of the divine;

4. *Catechism of the Catholic Church*, no. 460

it is only through treasuring our humanity that we can discover who God is. Of course it is difficult to believe such
good news and this is probably where we differ most of all
from Jesus. We think of ourselves as searching for God whereas
Jesus was consumed by the presence of the God who searches
for us but who finds the doors of our hearts closed, who cries
out to us but finds our ears are deaf, who surprises our eyes
with the beauty of the universe but who discovers that we are
blind, who dances before us in music and melody but who
finds that we are too lame to respond. The problem for Jesus
was not God's silence but humanity's hardened heart; it was
as if the divine song present in his heart could be heard by
nobody else. Thus it was that Jesus' ministry revolved
around the deaf, the blind, the lame, the crippled, the imprisoned, the dead. The reality of the human situation had
to be addressed if people were ever to hear the same tune
that Jesus heard or to see in human existence the miracle
that he saw.

According to the doctrine of the incarnation, God speaks
most powerfully through human life and experience. In order
to have any idea of the wonder and mystery of the incarnation, one must truly treasure one's own life. Nobody has highlighted this divine dimension of our lives more than Pope
John Paul II. Throughout his writings, and not least in *Tertio
Millennio Adveniente*, his encyclical looking forward to the
next millennium, one finds phrases like 'the human person is
the epiphany of God's glory,'[5] 'dwelling in the inmost life of
God,'[6] 'the Holy Spirit, who searches the depths of God,
leads us ... into these depths'.[7] These are beautiful words
which demand serious reflection rather than just a cursory
glance. Yet, even though phrases like this have been on the

---

5. Pope John Paul II, *Tertio Millennio Adveniente*, no. 6.
6. Pope John Paul II, *Tertio Millennio Adveniente*, no. 8.
7. Pope John Paul II, *Tertio Millennio Adveniente*, no. 8.

lips of Christians from the earliest times, I really wonder how many believers have ever plumbed their meaning.

There is no doubt but that for the earliest Christian believers these insights were the building blocks of their faith. In John's gospel the author is pushed to the limit to find language to express the intimacy of the God-human relationship. Ultimately he speaks of God setting up home in us humans. Imagine, we human vessels become the very homestead of the divine! Paul is overwhelmed by the presence of the Holy Spirit, the very Spirit of Jesus which turns us individuals into the body of Christ. In Romans 8 and Ephesians 3 Paul challenges us to journey into the inner reaches of our own lives in order to plumb the very depths of God. The key for both John and Paul was to be found in baptism and eucharist because in these two rituals the Spirit of God awakens us to the wonder of who we are and sows the seed of divinity in our hearts. Here then we see a critically important link between two key aspects of the life of the early Christian communities: belief in the incarnation and participation in the rituals of baptism and the breaking of bread. This linkage is encapsulated in the principle that Jesus is the sacrament of encounter with God, where the two meanings of the word 'sacrament' come together: (1) in Jesus the mystery *(sacramentum)* of God is revealed and (2) we encounter this mystery in the sacramental rituals of the church. The repetition of words is never sufficient to savour the depths of mystery; only symbol and ritual can touch and taste these broader horizons, and so it was that from the beginning it was in the ritual gatherings of the community that Jesus Christ, the mystery of God incarnate, was encountered.

Finally, we should acknowledge that belief in the incarnation is the distinguishing factor between Christianity and other world religions.[8] All major religions believe that the

8. Pope John Paul II, *Tertio Millennio Adveniente*, no. 6.

divine and the human are radically distinct from each other but only in Christianity does one find the God who enters fully into human life and raises it to share in the divine. That's why we speak of the Christian God as being a God of self-emptying, a God of *kenosis*. Although we humans and God remain really distinct, in Jesus of Nazareth divinity embraced humanity so completely that the two will never again be separated. This is the good news.

The church is the universal sacrament of salvation

Once we speak of Jesus as the primordial or original sacrament, it is only a short step to begin speaking of the church as sacrament. Again one can use any adjective one likes but the intention is the same: the church is not an eighth sacrament but one cannot understand the seven rites except as expressions of the faith of the ecclesial community. Nothing could lead to greater misunderstanding of the church's rituals than to cut them off from the evolving history of the believing community. That is why modern theology has devoted so much attention to the people, places and events of the first century, the era in which a new identity was chiselled out and expressed.

The soil in which the Christian faith of the first century grew was not that of rugged private individualism but rather the stony soil of newly emerging communities. Such communities are always, to one extent or another, in crisis. Imagine the texture of the group that formed around Jesus: women and men from rural Galilee, fishermen and tax collectors, hotheads and cynics, the scrupulously religious and the social outcasts. This was hardly fertile ground but it was among such as these that Jesus claimed the seeds of the kingdom of God were to be found, for these folk were the salt of the earth and the light of the world. Claims like these led Jesus to the cross; his motley crew of followers quite understandably disintegrated and scattered. What is truly incomprehensible, however, is the fact that they gathered again. In their writings, which came somewhat later, they tell us why: Jesus is alive; his Spirit is poured out amongst us; we encounter him; the tomb is empty; death couldn't hold him; we recognise him in the breaking of bread. So it was that the early communities were formed around faith in the resurrection.

We shouldn't romanticise these communities nor indeed the original group that formed around Jesus. The tendency is to interpret them in an overly pious way as if they lived lives radically different from our own. Nothing could be further from the truth. In Jerusalem, Antioch, Corinth, Thessalonika, Rome, Galatia and in countless other places, the earliest Christian communities were characterised by the same realities that are present in communal life throughout history: enthusiasm, tension, backbiting, fellowship, leadership, self-interest, jealousy, prophetic living. But what was most extraordinary about these communities was that, for all their limitations, they understood themselves to be the church, the *ecclesia* of God, the assembly of Yahweh, God's own people. From the rubble of Good Friday, God unlocked the tomb of human fear and limitation so that from Easter Sunday morning there emerged a people who 'are a chosen race, a royal priesthood, a consecrated nation, a people set apart to sing the praises of God who called you out of darkness into God's wonderful light. Once you were not a people at all and now you are the people of God' (1 Pet 2:9-10). The idea of the assembly was all important; when these people assembled for their ritual celebrations they were not just a group of individuals who happened to believe in God, but they were the body of Christ, the people of God. The later equation of the word 'church' with the building wherein Christians gather is deeply unfortunate, for the place where the people assemble is secondary. The church is the people who assemble, not the place where they assemble.

Over the first few centuries these assemblies of believers, particularly at the rituals of baptism and eucharist, affirmed the two central tenets of their new faith: the incarnation and the Triune nature of God. The latter was the hinge on which everything else turned. Though one could be forgiven for thinking otherwise, faith in the Trinity is at the very heart of Christianity. Throughout history the Triune nature of God has been ignored or subjected to the most abstruse philosophical-theological analysis or reduced to a mathematical conundrum. All such approaches ignore the affirmations of the early Christian communities: that the mystery of the divine is relational; that at the heart of God there is fellowship; that God's perfection is not reduced by but completed in relationship. Here we find ourselves at the frontiers of language; we cannot reduce God to our categories but we can use human language in a faltering way to speak analogously of the God revealed in Jesus of Nazareth. This God ceaselessly embraces what is other; the very life of God is in relation to the other and such relationship is completely self-emptying. In the act of creation God withdraws in order that the otherness of the cosmos might emerge. In the incarnation God embraces the otherness of humanity. On Calvary God is pushed out into the otherness of death. Through the resurrection God raises the otherness of human life into the sphere of the divine. In the out-pouring of God's Spirit humanity and the cosmos are being slowly drawn into God's future, a future characterised by relationship and otherness, for the life of God is all about relationship with the other. Prosaic language inevitably robs this mystery of its power; only in the heightened forms of human expression that we find in music, poetry, symbol and ritual can we encounter the relational dynamism of the Christian God.

The early Christians did not perceive God then to be individual but communal. It would be much easier to affirm God's absolute singularity, unity, isolation and transcendence as Judaism and Islam do. Instead the church follows the much more difficult path of affirming God's relationality in the doctrines of the incarnation and the Trinity. In order to express this mystery it speaks of one God in three divine Persons. This is not an arithmetical explanation but a sublime affirmation of what had been revealed in Christ. 'God is one but not solitary.'[9] Thus relationship, communality, otherness and difference are revealed in Jesus of Nazareth not only as human but also as divine realities.

It is commonplace today to hear people speaking highly of Jesus while denigrating the church; 'give me Christ but keep your church' is an oft heard refrain. Such a perspective is very attractive to the privatised religious spirit of our times but it has little to do with Christianity. Because God's own life is a shared communal one and the resurrection of Jesus created a community of faith, Christianity only exists in a communal context. To reduce Christian faith to personal religious sentiment is to reject the thought and action of the earliest Christian communities. However small or disorganised, however persecuted or comfortable, however strong or weak, however traditional or prophetic, however active or dormant, the community of believers is the primordial reality in Christianity. All else only makes sense as emerging from and existing for the community. The privatisation of life in general is one of the most insidious threats to Christian living today. The withdrawal into our living rooms where the television can become the key access to the world inevitably fragments the communal world that we once inhabited. The onslaught of the internet and cyberspace will offer opportunities for new types of cyber communities, where one's neighbour will not be defined geographically in terms of traditional space and time, but through virtual space and time. In this world of

9. *Catechism of the Catholic Church*, no. 254; see also nos. 253, 255 and 256.

technological revolution, sacramental space is squeezed and the interaction of community, religious belief and ritual is thrown into serious question.

Traditionally the parish has been the geographic focus of Christian community. Whilst it will continue to be so in rural and small urban settings, it is doubtful if geographical proximity is the key to community in the vast urban sprawls in which most of humanity will live in the future. In these new contexts, community tends to form around interests which are consumer driven. The Christian communities which emerge in the cities of the future will be counter-cultural, creating sacred sacramental spaces in the midst of urban anonymity, sowing the seeds of the kingdom of God in soil that appears hostile, subverting the cosy certainties of the consumer through liminal and *communitas* encounters. One thing is certain about such communities: they will not be a 'one man show' where all power is vested in the parish priest; there will be a plurality of ministries and it is probably the case that we will have to imagine new structures apart from parish to incarnate the church in the city.

Already, in the light of the Second Vatican Council, significant efforts have been made to renew the sacramental life of the church. Nowhere is this more obvious than in the sacramental language that we use. One can see definite contrasts in the language of the pre- and post-Vatican II liturgy:

Pre Vatican II	*Post Vatican II*
clerical centred	community
sacraments received	sacraments celebrated
passivity of recipient	faith of participant
rubric and law	word and symbol
priest is another Christ	a community in the Spirit
other-worldly	this-worldly
church centred	Christ centred
seven sacraments	sacramentality of all life

But although we have unquestionably changed the language, it is legitimate to ask whether very much else has happened. In fact, it could well be that in many parishes and other ecclesial contexts matters have ended up worse than they were in that the new language is used but the old reality persists. As ever in human life, when language and reality do not correspond tensions inevitably emerge. These begin with low levels of frustration, rising to significant experiences of alienation and finally to expressions of complete hostility. It would be a great tragedy if the spirit of the Council fails to move beyond language to create new realities. In order to do so, the law and theology which underpins the role of the parish priest will have to be developed towards new horizons of partnership and shared responsibility.

Be that as it may, the Christian community will always be a priestly community. It is easy to be clear about what this does not mean. It does not mean that everyone who is baptised is also ordained as a priest. The ministerial priesthood of word and sacrament remains distinct. But it does mean that all baptised Christians are called to share in the priesthood of Christ. They can do so in different ways but the ultimate goal is that the charisms freely bestowed by the Spirit of God should be placed at the service of all. From a Christian perspective, charisms or gifts are not just personal talents, they are intended for the upbuilding of the community. They vary enormously and are almost innumerable, but to give a flavour of how gifted the Christian community is, here are just a few: consoling the bereaved, healing the sick, comforting the lonely, encouraging the downcast, embracing poverty, reaching out to the addicted, being celibate, counselling, praying, leading, teaching, believing, hoping, loving. These charisms are present in abundance; it is the task of a priestly community to affirm them, to harness them and to challenge those that have been so gifted to put their gifts at the service of the Christian community. In this way the church becomes both a sign and an instrument of salvation; in other words, it becomes the universal sacrament of salvation.

The Second Vatican Council spoke many times of the church as the universal sacrament of salvation.[10] This means that the church is a sign and instrument of communion with God and unity amongst all people,[11] including those who appear to have no relationship with the church. The church exists to create this communion and unity. It can do so in different ways: praying, preaching, celebrating its rituals and, most powerfully of all, by building Christian communities which are themselves signs and instruments of this very communion with God and of unity amongst people. Such church communities will probably be smaller in the future but they will be characterised by those realities that have always been present in the church: prayer, a sense of mystery, healing, a feeling of belonging, reconciliation, ritual celebrations, prophetic critique of the values of the world. But one will also find sin, radical failure, narrow mindedness, stony hearts, abuse of power, alienation and cosy acceptance of consumerist values. In fact, the latter are at times so dominant that one wonders how the church could ever be a sign or an instrument of salvation. And yet it is and it must be because salvation is not just a private affair between me and my God but a radically communal reality based on the relational life of the Triune God and the assembly of God's people formed by the life, death and resurrection of Jesus of Nazareth. It is only in acknowledging the existence of blindness, egoism, hatred, pride, failure and sin that we can discover what salvation is, for it is from these realities that we must be saved. The church must face up to these

10. Most notably in *Lumen Gentium*: Dogmatic Constitution on the Church, no. 1; but also in *Lumen Gentium* no. 48 and *Gaudium et Spes*: Pastoral Constitution on the Church in the Modern World, no. 45.
11. See *Lumen Gentium* no. 1.

realities and open them to the healing and reconciling power of the gospel. When this is done by the people of God together, they become the universal sacrament of salvation.

To say that the church is the universal sacrament of salvation is not to say that all people must be members of the church if they are to be saved. It is in fact to say something very different. One of the most important changes in emphasis heralded at the Second Vatican Council concerned the salvation of those outside the church. No longer were they to be dismissed as insincere in their option for another religion or for no religion; instead it was acknowledged that ordinarily those who are not members of the church are in good faith. The Council clearly taught that those who live in accord with their consciences share intimately in the mystery of Christ. One could summarise the real revolution of the Second Vatican Council as a radical change in perception of those who do not belong to the church. Notice, for instance, that in the new Eucharistic Prayers the church community, gathered for its most important ritual, prays for all people. We pray for the living: 'Lord, may this sacrifice, which has made our peace with you, advance the peace and salvation of all the world,'[12] 'we offer you his body and blood, the acceptable sacrifice which brings salvation to the whole world,'[13] 'remember those who take part in this offering, those here present and all your people, and all who seek you with a sincere heart'.[14] And for the dead we pray: 'welcome into your kingdom our departed brothers and sisters and all who have left this world in your friendship,'[15] 'remember those who have died in the peace of Christ and all the dead whose faith is known to you

12. Eucharistic Prayer III.
13. Eucharistic Prayer IV.
14. Eucharistic Prayer IV.
15. Eucharistic Prayer III.

alone'.[16] Phrases like 'the whole world', 'sincere heart', 'your friendship' and 'known to you alone' echo the theology of *Lumen Gentium* 16 where in very prosaic language the church had affirmed the possibility of the salvation of all people. And in one of the most striking statements of the Council, it was acknowledged that 'since Christ died for everyone, and since all are in fact called to one and the same destiny, which is divine, we must hold that the Holy Spirit offers to all the possibility of being made partners, in a way known to God, in the paschal mystery'.[17]

There are crucial pastoral conclusions to be drawn from all of this. The days of dismissing everything outside the church – religions, rituals, traditions – as at best nonsense or at worst demonic, are over. Since salvation in Christ is historical, incarnate and communal, it is through the historical communities to which they belong that individuals encounter the mystery of Christ. This surely leads one to the conclusion that non-Christian religions and their rituals can be salvific. The Second Vatican Council's *Declaration on the Relation of the Church to Non-Christian Religions* says that:

> other religions which are found throughout the world attempt in different ways to overcome the restlessness of people's hearts by outlining a programme of life covering doctrine, moral precepts and sacred rites.
>
> The Catholic Church rejects nothing of what is true and holy in these religions. It has a high regard for the manner of life and conduct, the precepts and doctrines which, although differing in many ways from its own teaching, nevertheless often reflect a ray of that truth which enlightens all men and women … Let Christians, while witnessing to their own faith and way of life, acknowledge, preserve and encourage the spiritual and

16. Eucharistic Prayer IV.
17. *Gaudium et Spes* no. 22.

moral truths found among non-Christians, together with their social life and culture.[18]

There are also important implications for the inner life of the church in speaking of it as the universal sacrament of salvation. The church must be a sign and instrument of salvation not just for its own members but for all people. And since the church is most profoundly such a sign and instrument when the assembly of believers gathers for its sacramental celebrations, these very rituals should incarnate the church's concern for and its openness to the adherents of other religions and those who reject all religious faith. Thus the life of the church should never be constructed upon a narrow, sectarian, self-interested foundation which is preoccupied with its own preservation. Instead the church must devote its energy to becoming an authentic sign and effective instrument of salvation, of the life of God's Spirit which is encountered in healing, forgiveness, reconciliation, commitment and service. This suggests that Christian communities throughout the world should not worry too much about numbers or status but should focus their life and energy on becoming a sign and instrument of salvation for all people. This raises interesting questions for the celebration of the sacraments. Surely we should not be preoccupied with the numbers attending but, rather, our concern should be the quality of communal life among those who do participate. It is in the presence or absence of healing, forgiveness, reconciliation, commitment and service that the life of the church should be judged. We now know that such communal realities are not alone symbolised but are also activated through ritual. That is why ritual is a key to fostering an understanding of the church as the universal sacrament of salvation.

18. *Nostra Aetate*, no. 2.

The two rites of initiation in the Catholic Church

The rites of passage associated with initiation are amongst the most important in any culture or institution. These rites give a sense of belonging. They affirm one's identity whilst challenging one's commitment. They play a critically important role in fostering one's relationship with the community. Historically one can point to manifold examples of such rites which vary with the cultures in which they are found. But they tend to have much in common as demonstrated by Van Gennep's work. Childbirth and puberty become the focus for rites of passage through which one is initiated into the community, first as a child and then as an adult. The individual is no longer just a biological statistic but has embarked on the journey of becoming a person in a community. When these rites loose their force or indeed disappear altogether, then communities tend to atrophy and ultimately to die. The identity and life of the community is dependent upon the initiation of new members. Without this life-force created by the arrival of the neophytes, apathy, frustration and boredom supplant vitality, energy and hospitality. There is no more important question facing the Catholic Church at the dawn of the new millennium than how to breathe new life and energy into its rites of initiation. If they atrophy or descend to the level of empty cultural conformism, then the consequences for the church will be devastating. In looking to the future of Christian initiation we can learn much both from the early and recent history of the church. Modern historical and liturgical studies have produced voluminous material to reflect upon.[19] Such reflection might stir up possibilities of a new future for Christian initiation.

19. Detailed historical treatments include Liam G. Walsh, *The Sacraments of Initiation*, London: Geoffrey Chapman 1988; Aidan Kavanagh, *The Shape of Baptism: The Rite of Christian Initiation*, New York: Pueblo 1978; The Murphy Center for Liturgical Research, *Made, Not Born*, Notre Dame: University of Notre Dame Press 1976; Kenan B. Osborne, *The Christian Sacraments of Initiation*, New York: Paulist Press 1987.

From the very beginning, baptism was the rite of passage into the Christian community. The details of this rite evolved differently in the various Christian communities. One can trace this evolution through the Didache, written around 100 AD, and the writings of Justin Martyr (c. 100-165). But in the Roman tradition it is Hippolytus of Rome (170-235) who gives us the clearest picture of the nature of Christian initiation at the beginning of the third century. In summary, one can schematise the rite of Christian initiation detailed in Hippolytus' writings as follows:[20]

Catechumenate – up to three years in length.

Holy Saturday:
- anointing for exorcism
- profession of faith
- triple immersion
- anointing with chrism
- laying on of hands by bishop
- kiss of peace
- prayer of the faithful
- eucharist

The period of the catechumenate was a time of preparation before entry into the community. The one preparing for baptism was immersed in the scriptures, beliefs and traditions of the Christian church and introduced to the members of the local community. Baptised adults accompanied the catechumen on the spiritual journey from unbelief to faith. At the end of this period, the catechumen was brought before the community on Holy Saturday night for the rites of initiation. At this most solemn gathering, the catechumens, almost naked, were brought before a presbyter (priest) who anointed them with the oil of exorcism to strengthen their faith in the midst of evil and unbelief. With this oil dripping from their

20. For a more detailed description of the rite of Hippolytus, see Walsh, *The Sacraments of Initiation*, pp. 68-69.

bodies, they proceeded to the baptismal pool or font where, standing in the waters, they professed their faith in the Triune God and were immersed three times in the waters of baptism. Emerging from these life-giving waters, the newly baptised were anointed with chrism which gave them the fragrance of Christ himself. In an extraordinary prophetic act, the church poured the oil of chrism on their heads anointing them with the very Spirit of Jesus Christ. Drowned with water and covered in oil, the neophytes were brought before the bishop who laid hands on them while invoking the Holy Spirit to come upon them. Finally, they participated for the first time in the most intimate mystery of the life of the Christian community as they prayed with the faithful, shared the kiss of peace and were welcomed to the table for the breaking of bread where they encountered the greatest *sacra* of all as they ate and drank the body and blood of Christ. In the third century then, one sees a well developed ritual highlighting several key dimensions of Christian belief.

This ritual encapsulated the rich theology of baptism that emerged over the first few centuries of Christian belief. The baptised were immersed in the paschal mystery of the death and resurrection of Jesus (the christological effect); they became members of the church which is Christ's body (the ecclesiological effect); their sin was washed away (the soteriological effect); the Spirit of God was poured into their hearts as they became sharers in the very life of God (the pneumatological effect) and their future glory was anticipated (the eschatological effect). Just read over these effects again; this is awe inspiring stuff! There is no ritual in any tradition – polytheist, monotheist or secular – that makes such lofty claims. From 350-450 AD, in a century of unparalleled insights, bishops and theologians reflected ever more deeply upon the meaning of Christian initiation. But by the middle of the fifth century, the seeds of a much more limited model of initiation had been sown and they were to reap a harvest with very long term consequences.

The rite of initiation outlined above disintegrated for many different reasons. One might summarise them as follows:

(i) As a result of the change in the legal status of Christianity in the fourth century, huge numbers of people wanted to join the church. This flood of new members overwhelmed the catechumenate and resulted in an abbreviated form of preparation for initiation.

(ii) Augustine's theology of original sin raised the spectre of eternal damnation for all the non-baptised, even the infants of believers who died before being baptised. Such a scenario sowed the seeds of terrible fear in the hearts of sincere believers and fostered the idea of baptism as an emergency rite which should be completed *quamprimum,* as soon as possible, after childbirth.

(iii) But given these two serious developments, the church could have continued to initiate infants in accord with the traditions of Hippolytus and others. But a crucial question arose over the role of the bishop. In the Western church, bishops insisted on maintaining their role in the post-baptismal chrismation and the laying on of hands. With the exploding number of new members it proved impossible for the bishop to attend all initiation ceremonies. Babies were baptised locally; then they had to be brought to the bishop for the laying on of hands, in which he was literally confirming the earlier baptismal rite; at a later stage they were admitted to the table of the eucharist. So it was that the one continuous rite of initiation disintegrated into three distinct rites which we celebrate as the sacraments of baptism, confirmation and eucharist.

(iv) The ages at which these rites were celebrated varied throughout later history. Infant baptism became, and has remained, the norm in the Catholic Church. The rite that became known as confirmation was postponed and eventually wasn't celebrated until after one had reached the age of reason, traditionally seven years of age in Roman law. Some time later the individual was admitted to eucharist through receiving first holy communion. Thus the rite of initiation into the church followed the same pattern as earlier times except that it took approximately ten to twelve years to complete. But at the beginning of this century Pope Pius x, alarmed at the paucity of numbers receiving communion at ordinary Sunday Masses, sanctioned a new practice. In order to inculcate a habit of receiving holy communion from an early age, he reduced the age of admittance to first communion to seven. This had the desired effect in that over time a much larger proportion of those attending Sunday Mass frequently received communion. But Pius x's reform had a rather unfortunate side effect as it resulted in confirmation being postponed until after first communion. Thus the rite of initiation that existed in the early church was not only fragmented but also celebrated in a different order. This can be schematised as follows:

Infant Baptism	- anointing for exorcism
	- profession of faith
	- triple immersion
	- anointing with chrism
First Communion	- prayer of the faithful
	- eucharist
Confirmation	- anointing with chrism
	- laying on of hands by bishop
	- kiss of peace

The ordinary situation today in most countries is that those who are baptised as infants are admitted to first communion around seven or eight years of age and are confirmed at some point between eleven and fourteen years. One cannot give exact ages as the practice varies in different countries. This then is one rite of initiation in the contemporary Catholic Church.

There is also another quite distinct model of entry into the Catholic Church called the Rite of Christian Initiation of Adults (RCIA). This second rite emerged as a result of the Second Vatican Council where many bishops objected to the practice of initiating adults and children in the same manner, notwithstanding differences of age, maturity and personal expectations. So the Council requested a renewed rite for adults based on the practice of the early church.[21] The result was the RCIA which was first published in 1973. It re-established the catechumenate as a period of preparation for initiation during which one is introduced to the life of the Christian community through catechesis that centres on prayer, teaching, reading the scriptures, attendance at important liturgical gatherings and participation in works of service. In all of this, the role of the local community is crucial. The vision behind the RCIA is not one of a group of experts who prepare new members to join the church but rather of adults accompanying their sisters and brothers on a journey of faith. This journey is not just a matter of intellect but includes all aspects of life. When the period of the catechumenate draws to a close, the catechumen is initiated into the community. The crucial point is that they are not initiated in the same manner as infants, through three clearly distinguishable sacraments over many years, but in accord with the model of the early church outlined above. The community gathers to initiate new members, preferably at the Easter Vigil on Holy Saturday night. The ritual is then celebrated in much the same way as described by Hippolytus.

---

21. Second Vatican Council, *Sacrosanctum Concilium*: The Constitution on the Sacred Liturgy, nos. 64 and 66.

The theology that underpins the RCIA can be summarised in terms of:

- faith
- word
- community

The sacraments presuppose and nourish faith; without it they are meaningless. The RCIA challenges and affirms the faith of all involved in the process of initiation. The words of the scriptures must inform every sacramental celebration as they contain the story which the ritual enacts. The RCIA returns again and again to the structure of the church year and reflection upon the lectionary, so that the meaning of the scriptures unfolds in accord with the rhythms of time. The word should precede the sacrament; people must hear the good news before they celebrate it in ritual. But, maybe most importantly of all, there is a renewed emphasis on community. Initiation into the church is a deeply personal affair but it is not a private matter and so it should only be celebrated in a living community. The sacramental rituals exist not primarily for the comfort and encouragement of individuals but to create and sustain the life of the Christian community. Therefore, ordinarily they should be celebrated in a communal context. The sacraments exist not to provide us with private access to divine powers but to awaken us to the gift and responsibility of community. This is exactly what the RCIA attempts to do.

One can see, therefore, that there exist two distinct rites of initiation in the Catholic Church today – one for children and the other for adults. In comparing and contrasting the two methods of initiation there is much that one can learn. The following contrasts appear particularly apposite:

(a) The baptism of children became equated with the ablution of original sin to the neglect of all other effects of the sacrament. The RCIA highlights these other dimensions.

(b) In the popular imagination the baptism of children

was perceived to be an emergency rite intended to save the child from eternal loss. The RCIA is a process through which one is initiated into the Christian community.

(c) The link with Easter has long since been broken in the case of infant baptism. The retrieval of the paschal dimensions of Christian initiation is obvious in the RCIA with its renewed emphasis on Lent and Easter, particularly the Easter Vigil as the initiatory ceremony *par excellence.*

(d) Infant baptism has tended to become a private ceremony which does not involve the local Christian community in any vibrant way. The RCIA is a radically communal celebration which challenges the community to form and to welcome new members.

(e) Because of the dominance of infant baptism, initiation is understood more in terms of biology than ecclesiology: we baptise infants because they are infants and not because of any likelihood that they will be raised in the practice of the faith. The RCIA is premised on the never-ending journey of deepening faith as the shared belief both of the neophytes and the existing members of the community is affirmed and challenged through their mutual encounter.

One can see then that there are important differences between the two models of initiation presently operative in the Catholic Church. Given the significance of initiation in any living institution, these contrasts open up interesting avenues for further reflection in our efforts to revitalise and deepen the sacramental life of the church. In doing so, nothing is more important than to reflect on the paschal nature of Christian initiation, for the rite of passage – that is, entry into the church – must be paschal through and through.

The word 'pasch' has a rich history. It comes down to us in particular from the Jewish feast of Passover though it seems to pre-date even that ritual. In Palestine of old, nomadic peoples celebrated the spring lambing season with the sacrifice of a

yearling lamb in honour of the gods of fertility. In the story of
the Jewish exodus from Egypt the sacrifice of the lamb became salvific. Families were instructed to slaughter a lamb
and to sprinkle its blood on the lintels of their doors. Then
the first-born males would be saved from the destroying angel
who would pass over their houses. As a result of this plague
the Pharaoh released the Jews from slavery and they passed
over the Red Sea from slavery to freedom. Thus it was that
the people were saved by the blood of the innocent lamb,
known as the passover or paschal lamb, because the angel
passed over the houses and the people passed over the sea.
This became the great founding story of the Jewish people
and has been celebrated ever since in the annual feast of
Passover.

For the early Jewish Christians, Passover became central to
their self-understanding. Coming to terms with their belief in
the death and resurrection of Jesus, they turned to the Hebrew
scriptures to see if they could find some tradition that would
help to interpret what had happened. In the story of the
paschal lamb they found just such a tradition. As the blood of
the paschal lamb of old was shed, so Christians began to speak
of Jesus as the new paschal lamb through the shedding of
whose blood the people are saved. As the Jews passed over the
Red Sea so Christians would pass through the waters of baptism from slavery to freedom, from sin to forgiveness, from
death to life. And Christians had a new passover meal in their
eucharist. The early believers also looked to Isaiah 53 where
the innocent lamb bears the sins of the people as he is sent to
the slaughter. Thus it was that the lamb became one of the
first symbols of the newly emerging tradition.

In one of the earliest Christian documents, the First Letter
to the Corinthians, Paul says that 'Christ, our passover, has
been sacrificed' (1 Cor 5:7). In John's gospel the theme of the
paschal lamb is all important, as John the Baptist calls Jesus

the lamb of God (Jn 1:29) and Jesus died on the cross at the very time that the passover lambs were slaughtered in the temple for the Jewish feast. As he died on the cross, blood and water flowed from his side (Jn 19:34): blood – because Jesus is the new passover lamb through the shedding of whose blood the people are saved, and water – because new life comes from his death as the Spirit is poured out on the world through the waters of baptism.

This is why we speak of Christian initiation as entry into the paschal mystery of the death and resurrection of Jesus. It means that one is initiated into a discipleship of self-sacrifice; that one is immersed in the story and reality of Good Friday, Holy Saturday and Easter Sunday; that the life of the individual and the community must become cruciform and that, given the foretaste of the eucharist, we look forward to the final paschal meal where our cruciform nature will be liberated in the resurrection. It is into these paschal realities that the Christian is initiated, whether as a child or as an adult.

In this chapter we have analysed various strands in contemporary sacramental theology. These perspectives raise interesting questions concerning the renewal of Christian ritual. We will return to these in chapter six. In the meantime, we will turn our attention to a theologian who has not been mentioned so far but whose work constitutes an enriching new synthesis weaving together insights drawn from both traditional and contemporary sacramental theology.

The Contribution of Karl Rahner

Late have I loved you, O beauty ever ancient, ever new, late have I loved you. You were within me and I was outside and in my loneliness fell upon those lovely things that you have made. You were with me but I was not with you. I was kept from you by those things, yet had they not been in you, they would not have been at all. You called and cried to me and broke open my deafness, and you sent forth your light that shone upon me and chased away my blindness. You breathed fragrance upon me and now I pant for you, I tasted you and now hunger and thirst for you, you have touched me and now I burn for your peace.

St Augustine of Hippo, *Confessions*

The German theologian Karl Rahner has made his own indelible mark on our sacramental lives. Born in Freiburg in 1904 he entered the Jesuits in 1922. His philosophical and theological studies raised many questions about the nature of the human person, not least the issue of how human beings can possibly hear God's word and encounter the reality of God in their world. He began his teaching career in 1936 with a course on the theology of grace. Attempting to speak meaningfully about grace in the twentieth century became the fulcrum of his life's work. He was a key figure at the Second Vatican Council, pushing the church towards new horizons in her relationships with other Christian denominations, with

the different world religions and with non-believers. In the
1970s he was involved in various controversies over the selec-
tion of bishops, the appointment of professors of theology,
and what he perceived to be the loss of momentum in ecumenical endeavours. He died in 1984.

Like all other students of Catholic theology in the 1920s
and 1930s, Rahner was immersed in the neo-scholastic tradition. Neo-scholasticism was the generic term used to describe
the theology of the seminaries in the nineteenth and early
twentieth centuries. Over the years scholastic theology had
become formalised and decadent, enclosed in its own little
world and fearful of everything outside. At its worst, neo-
scholasticism was the theology of the ghetto which only made
sense within its own confines and was completely incapable
of engaging with the wider world. Its final flourish was the
anti-modernist crusade at the beginning of this century.
Rahner was deeply scandalised by the failure of this theology
to address many of the burning issues of his time such as dialogue with atheists, the challenges posed by human suffering,
the rising tide of personal freedom and democracy and last,
but by no means least, the call to Christian unity. Never one
to neglect the wellsprings of tradition, Rahner turned anew to
the great intellectual and pastoral riches of Catholicism to see
if it wasn't possible to construct a more open and dynamic
understanding of Christianity for our times. His achievement
was immense. We are still only scratching the surface in coming to terms with the implications of his thought. In no area
are these more radical than in our perception and practice of
the sacraments. To grasp the significance of his work one
must reflect on the nature of grace. It's interesting to remember that this was the first topic that Rahner taught and it
made an enormous impression upon him.

Neo-scholastic theology

What is grace? Neo-scholasticism spoke of grace as God's free gift which helped believers to overcome the effects of sin, formed good habits, sanctified those who received it and would ultimately bring them into God's blessed eternity. There were then different types of grace – justifying, habitual and sanctifying – which led one ultimately to the beatific vision, the face-to-face encounter with God. These graces built on nature, infusing it with a new power. Such grace, without which one could not be saved, was available only through the church and its sacraments. Therefore it was critically important to participate in the sacramental life of the church as those who did not, for whatever reason, were cutting themselves off from the very life of God. Rahner could see that there was much that was clearly edifying and true in these traditional perspectives, but he was disturbed by the institutional limitations which appeared to circumscribe God's encounter with humanity within the confines of the Catholic Church. This spurred him on to re-read the tradition in order to see if there was another way to interpret it. He discovered that indeed there was.

Traditionally theologians spoke of the two different realities of nature and supernature. The natural world of instinct and self-preservation has its own inherent law and dynamism but as a result of original sin it is overshadowed by human failure and limitation. The supernatural world of God exists beyond human consciousness and would remain unknown to us but that God has revealed it to us in Jesus Christ. As a result of this supernatural revelation, we become aware of our divine destiny and, through the sacramental life of the church, we receive the necessary grace to raise our fallen nature to its supernatural end. The problem with this understanding of the God-human relationship is that it suggests that the natural and supernatural worlds have essentially nothing in common, that they exist completely independently of each other, and that grace strikes the natural world as a force from without. Furthermore, this two-tiered universe suggests that human beings must renounce much of their natural humanity in response to their supernatural calling, as if coming to share in divine life was incompatible with a fully human existence. All of this is imaged in the great contrast of heaven and earth; now we struggle in a valley of tears but, through an ascetic penitential spirit and the gift of grace, we will be raised from this world to the blessed plenitude of heaven. Rahner was formed in the tradition of this thought. He read it and understood it but ultimately rejected it.

Re-interpreting tradition[1]

In re-reading the Catholic tradition, Rahner was struck by the absolute importance of the incarnation. The story of the incarnation was not just one of a divine messenger who issued decrees and demanded that we live in a certain way, but was rather the story of the transformation of humanity from within. God did not just reach down from a supernatural world to give some ideas and instructions to human beings on how to escape the limitations of their humanity. In the person of Jesus Christ, God laid hold of human nature and justified and divinised it. This understanding was expressed in the early church's belief in the divine in-dwelling. St Paul spoke eloquently of the Spirit of God living within us and amongst us (Rom 5:5; 8:9, 11, 15, 23; 1 Cor 3:16; 6:19; 2 Cor 1:21-22; 3:3; Gal 4:6-7), whilst St John was consumed by the presence of the

1. Rahner's key writings on grace are: 'Concerning the Relationship Between Nature and Grace' and 'Some Implications of the Scholastic Concept of Uncreated Grace' in *Theological Investigations Volume 1*, London: Darton, Longman & Todd, pp. 297-346; 'Reflections on the Experience of Grace', in *Theological Investigations Volume 3*, London: Darton, Longman & Todd, pp. 86-89; 'Nature and Grace' in *Theological Investigations Volume 4*, London: Darton, Longman & Todd, pp. 165-188.

Triune God who sets up home in us (Jn 6:56; 14:16-20, 23; 17:26; 1 Jn 3:24; 4:12-16). In other words, what happened in Jesus of Nazareth was not just the offer of new information or a new vision or a new understanding of the world but the gift of God's own life. This is why Rahner endlessly speaks of grace as God's self-communication in Christ.

Our human nature has been transformed by the grace of Christ, so much so that there is no longer a two tiered universe of nature and supernature but the natural world of humanity already bears the seeds of its supernatural destiny. This type of thought gave rise to another one of Rahner's key phrases – the human being as the supernatural existential. Although un-questionably an off-putting term, what it claims is all import-ant: that as a result of the life, death and resurrection of Jesus Christ the existence of every human being, believer and non-believer alike, has a supernatural destiny and that the seeds of divinity are already present in every human life.

These are the insights behind Rahner's theology. The past-oral and personal implications are manifold. Our supernatural end is no longer to be understood purely in terms of other-worldliness but also as an inner journey to the very depths of our own humanity in which we encounter divinity. God is re-vealed not only in the words of scripture and the life of the church but also in personal human experience. In the human journey of each person there are experiences which are power-fully revelatory (epiphanies) of who we are and what we are called to become. These are particular moments (kairoi) which stand out against the general flow of time (chronos) which is eminently forgettable. Although it is arrogant to pre-suppose that one can list such experiences, as they are sure to vary from one person to another, one can identify some which seem to transcend the boundaries of all cultures: unex-pected joy, discontent with material things, the heartbreak of bereavement, loneliness, forgiveness, laughter and tears, failure and breakdown, hoping against hope, silence and, most powerfully of all, the unmerited love of another. These *kairos* experiences break through the narrow horizons we often inhabit and open us up to the mysterious and incomprehensible nature of our humanity.

We dwell in mystery. Between womb and tomb most of our lives are spent in routine repetition but now and again, usually unexpectedly, we are forced out to the edge, the limit, the threshold, from where we see things in a new way. These are graced moments, invitations to surrender ourselves to the mystery which envelops us. Rahner speaks of God as Holy Mystery. God is not the answer to all our problems but the One who invites us to ever new horizons. Christians should not perceive the boundaries of their knowing, loving, hoping and believing as limitations but as horizons. An horizon is the furthest point we can see from where we are standing now. Horizons are not tragic limitations but open invitations. At the furthest horizons of human consciousness all we can do is surrender in silence to the mystery of God's own future. God is not a concept in our heads but the One we encounter yet cannot grasp at the horizon of our knowing and loving, laughing and crying, hoping and believing. These are encounters with grace which transcend our ordinary experience, yet challenge us and enable us in our day-to-day lives to stand by the truth, to overcome egoism, to forgive, to give in self-sacrifice, to follow one's conscience, to be faithful, to hope and to love. Grace then does not exist as some other-worldly quantifiable material which is poured into our souls but as the call to and the reality of self-transcendence which is the very soul of human life. Rahner comments:

> One thing must be emphasised about this grace precisely as emerging from the inmost centre of man and the world. It does not occur as a particular phenomenon alongside the rest of his life, as a special process. Grace is simply the

last depth and the radical meaning of all that the created person experiences, enacts, and suffers in the process of developing and realising himself as a person.[2]

Thus, if we are truly to grasp the meaning of grace, there is much to be learned from reflection upon our own human experience. What most disturbed Rahner about traditional scholastic theology was its inability to speak meaningfully to ordinary human experience.

Let's now repeat a question that we asked earlier: what is grace? This time we will answer it from Rahner's perspective. The word 'grace' is a translation of the Greek word *charis* meaning gift. As ever, Rahner would like us to turn to human experience to determine what this word really means. To this end it is interesting to follow the next three steps: (1) to analyse the human phenomenon of bestowing gifts (to test the veracity of what emerges, just compare it with any example of sincere offering and receiving of gifts in your own life); (2) to apply this analysis to traditional claims concerning grace and (3) to accept human life itself as grace.[3]

(1) Analysing the human phenomenon of bestowing gifts

(a) The receiver does not have to earn the gift; if that were the case then it would be a wage.

(b) Gifts are not in the control of the recipient since the generosity of the giver cannot be circumscribed.

(c) A true gift does not seek recompense; if it does, then it is not a gift but a bribe.

(d) The worthiness of the recipient is not important; those who offer gifts do so purely because they want to bestow the gift upon the other.

2. Karl Rahner, 'A Copernican Revolution: Secular Life and the Sacraments', in *The Tablet*, 6 March 1971, p. 237.
3. What is being attempted in these three steps is a phenomenology of gift rather than an ontology of grace.

(e) Gifts sincerely offered to the other either deepen existing relationships or set up new relationships.

(f) The greatest form of giving is undoubtedly self-giving.

(2) Applying these conclusions to traditional claims concerning grace

If we now apply these six aspects of human giving to the traditional theology of grace we will see how strongly our own experience echoes in this theology.

(a) God's grace is freely given and never earned by human beings.

(b) The initiative always rests with God as humans cannot control God's generosity.

(c) Grace is given whether human beings respond or not.

(d) Human sin and failure do not destroy God's gift; grace is bestowed not because humans are worthy but because God is loving.

(e) Through grace we enter relationship with God.

(f) The greatest grace is to share in God's own life.

These two steps demonstrate that there is much in the nature of human giving and receiving which is mirrored in what Christians have traditionally said about God's grace. But remember that Rahner's most important claim is that human life itself is graced. We now have criteria drawn from human experience and Christian tradition which can be used to look at human life as God's gift.

(3) Accepting human life as grace

(a) We find ourselves thrown into life. It takes an act of faith to accept our lives as a gift rather than a burden or a test or a freak biological accident.

(b) Life is not in our control even though we lose a lot of energy trying to control it. No human beings ever determine the most important facts in their lives, as individuals have no choice concerning parents, siblings, the when and where of their birth or their childhood experiences. We are asked to take all of this on trust, to receive it as a gracious gift.

(c) Human life is a gift, not a bribe or a test.

(d) We do not have to prove ourselves worthy to be alive. Accepting life as gift liberates us from the tyranny of ceaselessly seeking the approval of others in order to convince ourselves that we are valuable and lovable. There is an original doubt deep in all of us which suggests that our lives are of no real value and that nobody could love us; only an act of faith in life's giftedness can free one from this inner temptation to despair.

(e) Through the grace that is human life, whether we fully appreciate it or not, all of us are in relationship, with others, with the universe and with the mystery called God.

(f) Because of Jesus Christ human life is not only God's gift but it is also an invitation to share in the mystery of God's own life.

To accept life in this way demands an act of faith. But even if individuals reject such faith as false or maybe even impossible, based on their experience of life, the potential still remains to accept God's revelation of life as gift. God's 'yes' is greater than any human 'no'.[4] Gift comes before response and grace comes before freedom. If one truly believes this, then preaching is not just propaganda but a word that might reveal something of the wonder and value of who we are; catechesis is not just information but a spark that might ignite the seeds of divinity present in all humanity; prayer is not just empty repetitions but an invitation to embark on the longest journey, the journey inwards; dialogue with adherents of other religions and of none is not just human courtesy but a light that might create a new future based on true respect; humanising

4. Karl Rahner, *Foundations of Christian Faith*, New York: Crossroad, 1993, p. 412.

the world and its social structures is not just a political goal but a divine imperative that might allow all people to savour their own uniqueness. But of course the important question remains – what then of the sacraments? What do we make of the sacraments in this scheme of things?

A 'Copernican Revolution'

The simplest summary of traditional theology is that the sacraments give grace. The ordinary believer goes to Mass or one of the other sacraments to receive that grace which is not otherwise available. Therefore the more often one goes the better. But to many people today, believers and non-believers alike, such an approach to religious expression appears at best unreal and, at worst, magical. Rahner comments:

> The sacraments get suspected of being nothing else but an empty ritualism. The impression is easily given in this traditional approach that the sacraments and the Mass 'do not help', cannot really change anything in life: it is felt that after Mass everything goes on in exactly the same way as it did before, just as it does in fact without Mass. The 'devout' person might still insist on the religious experiences the sacraments provide him with, the 'consolation' and strengthening they give him, but the not so 'devout' person will see in this attitude the very thing he rejects, namely a flight from the rigour of real life into an ideological world of unreality.[5]

The danger is that those who participate in the sacraments can equate their religious belief with attendance at sacramental rituals, while those who have lapsed from sacramental practice can belittle the whole process as magic or escapism. The former risk reducing religion to ritual while ignoring the challenge to values and lifestyle; the latter are tempted to re-

5. Karl Rahner, 'A Copernican Revolution: Secular Life and the Sacraments',
p. 237.

ject religious ritual in the embrace of a privatised belief system. Both of these trends need to be challenged. Rahner characterised the change required in our sacramental understanding as akin to a copernican revolution.

The first reality that one must affirm is the presence of grace in our lives and our world.

The world is penetrated and filled with God's grace. The sacraments are certainly events of this grace in its forgiving, sanctifying and divinising power. Yet this must not be understood as though the world were otherwise profane and without grace, only to be struck as it were from without by divine grace at the moment of the sacramental act.[6]

The key question is not whether grace exists but whether the individual will accept it or reject it. Only if one accepts that life itself is grace do the sacraments make any sense; otherwise they will inevitably appear to be a flight from reality into a world of magic and illusion. The sacraments are like signs raised in the world affirming the holiness and divine significance of our secular lives.[7] The true liturgy is the liturgy of the world with its pain and joy, heartbreak and love, betrayal and promise, tedium and insight, death and life. In plumbing the depths of these realities we learn something of the presence of grace, of the drama of gift and response, of grace and sin. The seven sacraments must be rooted in this drama of our lives where our divine destiny is encountered, often ignored or rejected, sometimes embraced and cherished. Those who believe that grace and divinity do not touch human life should steer well clear of the sacraments, for they are sure to appear to them as nothing more than the worst forms of escapism and magic.

6. Karl Rahner, 'A Copernican Revolution: Secular Life and the Sacraments', p. 237.
7. Karl Rahner, 'Secular Life and the Sacraments: The Mass and the World', in *The Tablet*, 13 March 1971, p. 267.

When we go to the sacramental rituals, that which is already happening in the world in terms of redemption and hope is brought to consciousness, celebrated and enacted. We shouldn't underestimate how significant this is for, in the ordinary routine of life, our experience of grace is often anonymous and might make little impact upon us. The seven sacraments should be a celebration of the world as revealed in the life, death and resurrection of Jesus: a beautiful, mysterious world rent assunder by violence, hatred and egoism but already bearing the fruit of redemption and the seeds of divinity. To attend the sacraments is not to seek escape from the reality of life or to turn away from the world, but rather it is to cherish the gift of life, to turn towards the world and to celebrate light in the midst of deepest darkness.[8]

The sacramentality of life

Thus it was that Rahner rooted the sacramental rituals in the ordinary experience of human life. His work raises the possibility of rediscovering the sacramentality of life in the light of modern theological insights. Traditionally, a sacrament was defined narrowly as one of seven rites instituted by Christ and properly administered by the church. More broadly today, in the light of Rahner's reflections, one might begin to speak of the sacramentality of any human experience of salvation in the world or in history, for any such experience is an integral part of salvation in Jesus Christ. Both of these perspectives are useful but limited. The broad one seems to lack any focus while the narrow one fails to give due weight to personal experience. The two might be combined as follows: the goal of Christian communal living is to walk the journey together, to encounter the Lord in the sacramentality of life and

8. See Karl Rahner, *Meditations on the Sacraments*, London: Burns & Oates, 1977.

to celebrate our Christian identity in the seven rites instituted by Christ and properly administered by the church.

Today then we are leaving behind an older mindset which believed that grace was only accessible through the seven rituals of the church, and embracing Rahner's perspective that grace has laid hold of nature and begun to transform it from within. As a result, grace is active in our lives and our world before, during and after the sacramental event. Therefore, we must accept the paradoxical truth 'that grace is always at work from within and nevertheless also comes from without through the particular time-bound intervention of the sacramental sign.'[9]

9. Karl Rahner, 'Secular Life and the Sacraments: The Mass and the World', p. 268.

Passage to Pasch[1]

O chestnut-tree, great-rooted blossomer,
Are you the leaf, the blossom or the bole?
O body swayed to music, O brightening glance,
How can we know the dancer from the dance?

W. B. Yeats, *Among School Children*

We are only the earthenware jars that hold this treasure, to
make it clear that such an overwhelming power comes from
God and not from us.

St Paul, 2 Corinthians 4:7

In previous chapters we have analysed the nature of ritual, situated this analysis in particular aspects of the Irish context, studied in some detail traditional and modern approaches to the Catholic sacraments and, finally, interrogated the work of Karl Rahner to see what light it might shed on these issues. It has emerged that ritual and symbol are crucially significant in any meaningful understanding of human personhood; that rites of passage are common to all cultures; that rites of initiation are the most important rites of passage; that people resort easily and frequently to fertility rites; that such rites can demean our humanity and enslave us to magic; that the history of religion has been blighted by the zealous destruction of

---

1. Some of the material used in this chapter has been published in 'A Ritual Question', in *The Furrow*, Vol. 45, 1994, pp. 141-150.

symbol and ritual as religious adherents, particularly of monotheistic faiths, violently destroy all vestiges of fertility rites; that the insights and wisdom of the Catholic sacramental tradition are worthy of respect and reflection; that Christian initiation into the fellowship of believers and discipleship of Christ must be renewed; that such renewal must take place in the context of a deepened sense of the presence of grace in our world.

We live in a broken world. Illness and death, violence and fear, hatred and despair, poverty and hunger, stalk our world. How to speak a word of healing and hope in the midst of life's most abject experiences is the task of Christian living. Cheap words which offer pathetic solutions to life's most inscrutable problems, or that deny the pain that many endure, are useless. Oftentimes there is little that is worth saying and in our wordlessness all we can do is cling to faith, hope and love, facing the silence and solitude with what grace we can. Helping people to rebuild broken lives is the goal of Christian faith. Jesus came to bring good news to the poor, liberty to captives and healing to the deaf, the dumb, the blind and the lame. We are the poor, the captive, the deaf, the dumb, the blind and the lame, not in some analogous spiritual sense but in the personal, psychological, political and religious reality of our lives. That is why human life is not about perfection; it is all about redemption.

In order then to treasure the real meaning of redemption, we must face up to our own very definite limitations. Due to the seeds of self-doubt and fear (traditionally called original sin) that are found in all of us, and which have the capacity to reap a harvest of paranoia, pride and prejudice, we often fail to appreciate the truth and beauty of who we are in God's eyes. And so we need to be redeemed before we can delve into the divine presence in our own humanity. We need healing, since we can become deaf through routine, blind through pride, lame through tragedy, crippled by prejudice, imprisoned by fear, and dead spiritually even if not physically.

In the Advent liturgy we celebrate the coming of God into the world. It is in life's wilderness that the way of the Lord must be prepared. We must face right into the middle of this wilderness if we are to fill in the valleys, lay low the mountains and make the cliffs a plain. God's coming is always as bread to the hungry, comfort for the sorrowful, healing for the afflicted, hope for the despairing and forgiveness for the sinner. In other words, it is always redemptive.

The nature of Christian redemption is paschal. According to Christian belief all humanity must follow Christ through the mystery of death and resurrection. The paschal dimensions of our experience are numerous as we must continuously let go in order to develop and grow. In our birth we had to let go of the security of our mother's womb and emerge into a strange world; in adolescence we let go of the innocence of childhood; all of us have to let go of home, parents must let go of their children and children must let go of their parents; throughout life as we grow and mature we must continually let go of opinions, jobs, good health and ultimately of the idea that we are in control and, of course, in death we must let go of those we love. Between womb and tomb life is an endless process of letting go. Life is the greatest gift we have received and we must, in the end, even let go of this gift. We must let go of the past to let God be the God of the future.

Depending on what happens in these various passages, we grow in self-love or, tragically, in self-hatred. All of us are tempted to inner despair; we can be overcome by self-doubt and fear. We need to hear the word of redemption that we are indeed loved, that our lives are valuable, that we are cherished. This word must come from without, for if we only repeat it to ourselves then we could never be sure that it isn't an illusion. The main function of Christian ritual is to speak such a word to us. In order to do so, our rituals must become paschal, incarnating both the reality of our brokenness and the divine gift of healing and redemption.

To make our rituals truly paschal is a never ending struggle. It echoes the ancient journey from polytheism to monotheism. But as this was the way that religions historically evolved, so it is the path that individuals must tread in their own lives. It is easy to dismiss the adherents of primitive religions and their fertility rites, but in reality we have much more in common with them than we care to admit. At a personal level, placing one's trust in God alone instead of depending on the false gods of ego, wealth, security or status is a life-long effort.[2] Given that we often worship these gods, we should be slow to condemn primitive religious rituals.

The task of translating all our human passages into expressions of Christ's paschal mystery remains. When one looks again at some of the threads that have been weaved together in this book, three principles can be formulated concerning the paschal character of ritual.

(1) To be truly paschal ritual must move from magic to prophecy
In chapter two we schematised the relationship of magic and prophecy as follows:

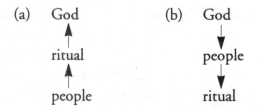

Scheme (a) is magic as it enslaves people to ritual; (b) is prophetic as it liberates people to celebrate their identity in

2. The struggle to move from polytheism to monotheism forms an important part of James W. Fowler, *Stages of Faith*, San Francisco: Harper & Row, 1981.

ritual. Once one keeps in mind that the people are primordial
and the rituals are secondary then one will avoid the danger of
ignoring the plight of the people while insisting on the divine
significance of the ritual. The realities of violence, injustice,
hunger, social exclusion and racism must be acknowledged
and challenged in all Christian ritual. To ignore these and
hope that participation in the ritual will somehow solve our
problems is the most objectionable form of magic. Ritual will
not solve any of the great questions we face. We must take responsibility for ourselves, for all people and for our planet.
Christians have a special responsibility, given their faith in
Christ and appreciation of human life as God's self-gift. The
sacraments are all important since they should affirm our
identity and challenge us to become what we are called to be.
Understood in this way, the sacraments are not escapes into
the realm of magic but prophetic actions celebrating the past
and anticipating the future.[3]

One of the great sources of renewal in the church has always come from the edge, the margins. From there voices of
prophetic critique have been raised calling the church to reform itself. In the language used earlier in this work, people
withdraw from the ordinary structures of human society to
live on the periphery where they experience the liminal and
communitas in a more vibrant way.[4] Historically, religious orders often performed this service; today such radical voices
are critically important since the church is ever tempted to
become nothing more than a prop for the dominant political
system. Its rituals will only be renewed when *communitas*
resurges once more from liminal spaces.[5] Such rituals today

3. The issues raised in this paragraph are analysed in great depth and with exem-
plary clarity in Eamonn Bredin, *Praxis and Praise*, Dublin: Columba Press 1994.
4. Eamonn Bredin uses Victor Turner's category of *communitas* to interpret Jesus'
ministry in *Disturbing the Peace*, Dublin: Columba Press, 1985, pp. 137-164.
5. See Carl F. Starkloff SJ, 'Church as Structure and Communitas: Victor Turner
and Ecclesiology' in *Theological Studies*, Vol. 58 (1997), pp. 643-668.

will have to open people to the liminal, awakening a sense of the numinous and the mysterious, stirring the great powers of wonder and awe, creating small dynamic communities where people feel wanted and cared for, whilst affirming and challenging commitment.

In the future the church in many countries will be much smaller, more akin to leaven in the world rather than a massive institution. Such a church will have to depend much more on the quality of its communal life as cultural supports disappear. In such a context, the rite of passage which is initiation will become ever more important. Victor Turner's understanding of ritual as separation, liminality and reaggregation offers many possibilities for recasting Christian initiation so as to emphasise its paschal, prophetic nature. Such a task is one of the most important facing the church as the Christians of the future will have to learn how to live on the margins in liminality and *communitas*.

Already major efforts have been made to renew Christian initiation. From 1968-73 the Vatican Congregation for Divine Worship produced revised rites for all the sacraments. Those involved in this process placed enormous emphasis on the most important rite of passage in the church – that of initiation into the church through baptism, confirmation and eucharist. As a result, two of their most important pastoral revisions were the Rite of Christian Initiation of Adults (RCIA) and a renewed rite for the Easter Vigil as the initiation celebration *par excellence*. The RCIA held out great hope for renewal but it hasn't worked because the creativity and ritual expression on which it is premised haven't flourished. What is required is the creative use of imagination and faith to continually ritualise the wonderful and awe-inspiring claims of sacramental initiation. An imaginative sensitivity to symbol and ritual should be fostered among those preparing for ordination as priests so that when they come to preside at the sacraments they might facilitate creativity and openness to mystery.

The efforts to renew the Easter Vigil are particularly instructive. The ceremony is well thought out in terms of word, action, movement and symbol, yet, in contrast to ecclesial events of much lesser significance like the blessing of throats or distribution of ashes or pilgrimage to a Marian shrine, it is poorly attended. Look at baptism in general: it is perceived as central in theology, official pronouncements and pastoral planning, but it has made no such impact on the popular mind. I have often asked adult groups to name the central Christian symbol of Easter – the responses include eggs, flowers, spring, longer evenings, candles, crosses; one seldom hears mention of the lamb and never of baptism! Surely this much teach us something about the renewal of ritual? Have we gone too far too fast? Or maybe we didn't go in the right direction at all?

One of our most basic errors has been to ignore the story of our people. We must learn to trust our own experience as initiated Christians. God's Spirit has been poured into our hearts and we are part of God's word to the world – we need to express this in our rituals. How? Could we read, at least occasionally, non-biblical texts? Could we begin to hear the voice of the bereaved at funerals? Could we encourage couples to express their ministerial role at the marriage ceremony? Could we gather, apart from the seven sacraments, in warmth and peace to sing and pray and witness and listen to who we are? Could we, in the spirit of the RCIA, have freedom to adapt the liturgy to the life and contemporary experience of our local communities so that we rejoice with those who rejoice, weep with those who weep, struggle with those who struggle and hope against hope with those who despair? The value of all of these is that we could enhance our people's sense of belonging to a particular community, which is precisely what the RCIA and the revised Easter Vigil presume. But the presump-

tion is, at least to some extent, false. We have many initiated
folk (having celebrated the sacraments of baptism, confirmation and eucharist) who do not feel that they belong. If we are
truly to focus our rituals on prophecy rather than on magic,
then we will have to shift people's religious consciousness
from individual salvation to communal responsibility. Only
in this way can the paschal significance of the passage that is
initiation be retrieved for our times. Turner's theory of ritual focussing on separation, liminality and *communitas,* when
combined with a retrieval of the significance of Easter in
Christian life, raises interesting possibilities for the paschal renewal of the passage of initiation.

(2) To be truly paschal ritual must be inculturated

Inculturation is an important concept in contemporary
theology. It refers to the mutual interface of faith and a particular culture. In this book we have studied the Irish cultural
context. The Christian faith has become inculturated in
Ireland over two millennia to such an extent that the faith and
the culture are inseparable. And what an interesting mix it is
of traditional religion and Christian doctrine, where many of
the folk believe in both the Trinity and fairy forts, where belief in transubstantiation and holy wells exist side by side,
where many of the great feasts are as pagan as they are
Christian, where the priest has many of the powers of the
druid. Brian Friel has dramatised the power and paradox of
our rich tradition and, while it will at times offend doctrinal
purity, it is a tradition that has lived and thrived. Inculturation does not mean adopting the latest cultural fad (like
the nonsense of suggesting that we replace bread and wine in
the eucharist with cola and crisps) but that we allow the archaic symbols and rituals of a particular culture to be expressed anew. Archaism is all important in ritual, as ancient
symbols have the power to evoke a sense of the sacred, a sense

of our *communitas* with the dead, with the past and with the earth. In Ireland we have potent archaic traditions – like pilgrimage, fasting, station Masses, funeral wakes – which could make a significant contribution to the renewal of our sacramental lives. The value of archaic rituals and symbols in any culture is that they are home brew and so they find an echo deep in the sub-conscious of the people.

The seven sacraments celebrate God as Creator, Redeemer and Sanctifier. This is a wonderful ritual tradition of worship of the one true God before whom we bow rather than reason. But maybe we reason too much. Our church rituals are too cerebral and verbal. As we participate in these ancient rituals we must be creative; our forebears certainly were. Archaism and creativity go hand in hand. Many believers are turning to what is called 'creation-centred spirituality' in order to ritually express their faith anew. They are doing so because, quite literally, they find it more creative in terms of atmosphere, silence, movement and celebration of the sacred. In today's world, increasingly dominated by Anglo-American television culture, we must face serious questions about how we will ritualise God's presence in our midst. Obviously, for Catholics, the seven sacraments will remain the key means of evoking and celebrating the sacred. But Catholics have always known that we also need more than the sacraments when it comes to ritualising and symbolising our faith. Rites which celebrate personal development, the discovery of the indwelling God, the endless horizons of the inner life, the social and political demands of the gospel, will be important in the future and will probably supplant many of the pious exercises which were common over the past century. Whatever the future holds, Irish Catholics should not be afraid when it comes to inculturating faith because we belong to the richest ritualising institution the world has ever known and we are descendants of a people who ceaselessly expressed their faith in ever-changing rituals.

Three threads from the arguments presented in this book are particularly pertinent to inculturation. We saw in chapter two the difficulties that were created in Galatia when it was suggested that accepting the gospel also meant embracing a foreign culture. Unfortunately this has happened time and again throughout history but it has nothing to do with true Christianity; it is in fact the forces of cultural hegemony and political oppression that are at work. Embracing the gospel never demands that people renounce their culture and traditions but that the seeds of the gospel already present be nourished and fostered so that the form of Christ's pasch might emerge. In chapter three, the church's teaching that the sacraments bestow grace *ex opere operato*, by the performance of the rite, was analysed. It became clear that while this is an important principle it does not rule out the possibility that other rituals can also bestow grace; indeed it would almost seem to imply this. The study of Rahner's theology in chapter five pointed to the presence of grace in all human life and therefore in all cultures. Given the significance of rites of passage in every tradition, the process of inculturating the Christian message must involve focussing these passages on their paschal goal. To be truly paschal, ritual must be inculturated because people are born into various cultures and traditions and it is through these that the Holy Spirit unfolds the paschal mystery.

(3) To be truly paschal ritual must incarnate memory and hope
    In the broken, messy world that we inhabit, celebrating Christian ritual is like erecting a sign that speaks of memory and hope. The two most important things that an individual ever says are: 'I remember' and 'I hope'. When these words lose their meaning, life unravels as our links with the past and the future are severed. Nobody can survive long in such a vacuum – they will turn to fashion or drugs or ambition or suicide to numb the pain in facing an intolerable future.

Christian ritual incarnates memory and hope. In baptism the church anticipates its hope in the future while celebrating its ancient faith. This emphasis on the future is all important. Liam Bergin comments: 'When the ecclesial community celebrates the sacramental rite, it unveils in the present the power of the future ... by re-enacting the prophetic action, the future, which is signified in it, is grafted into the present experience of the worshipping community.'[6] The most significant moment in the future of each person is his or her death. Terry Eagleton comments on the baptism of a baby boy:

> the first major appointment in his diary has to be with death, which will also of course be his last one. His entrance into the world has somehow to anticipate his exit. If he's to have any chance at all of living well in a crucifying world, he'll have to start off by giving himself away, descending into the waters of baptism ...[7]

Our baptismal lives take shape in the space opened up between memory and hope. Memory gives us a sense of who we are, and hope ceaselessly challenges us to renounce our self and sectional interests in an effort to anticipate the future which is God's promise. Without memory and hope we are only scraps of biology blown hither and thither. Our rituals, particularly baptism, must awaken us to the paschal significance of our passage from womb to tomb.

During that passage, meals of fellowship will nourish and encourage us. If we never eat and drink with family and friends we will never hear the stories of where we come from or foster the inner strength and hope to face what the future might bring. For Christians the eucharist is food for the journey, not an escape hatch into a world of unreality. The first

6. Liam Bergin, 'O Propheticum Lavacrum': Baptism as Symbolic Act of Eschatological Salvation, Rome: Gregorian University Press, 1998, p. 189.
7. Terry Eagleton, 'Homily for Oliver's Baptism', in The Furrow, Vol. 48, 1997, p. 419.

name for the eucharist was the breaking of bread. As the disciples recognised the Lord in the breaking of bread so they and their successors would have to learn how to recognise him in the brokenness of life.

The eucharist is the ultimate paschal ritual. When Jesus said, 'Do this in memory *(anamnesis)* of me', he was giving an explicit command to his followers to celebrate his memory through ritual. Such memory is not just an intellectual act of recollection but an encounter once more with the mystery of Christ's self-giving in death. When we gather for the eucharist we are also looking forward in hope. Dermot Lane comments:

> In particular the eucharist captures *in embryo* the future transformation of the cosmos into a New Creation. The material elements of bread and wine are transformed into the Body of Christ, reminding us that material creation itself is destined to be part of the New Creation in Christ ...
> The eucharistic assembly is that particular historical location on earth that seeks to symbolise in word and sacrament the dreams and hopes released by Jesus for the future of humanity and creation.[8]

This is why, in the end, Christians must be iconophile rather than iconoclast, for the whole of creation is itself an icon of God's presence. In Christ we have the fulness of God's self-gift and in return we offer bread and wine – fruit of the earth and work of human hands. Through some of the most basic and simultaneously the most wonderful of human creations – bread and wine – divinity becomes most intimately present to humanity.

On our passage from womb to tomb we need symbols and rituals to keep hope and memory alive so that we do not lose sight of our paschal origins or our paschal destiny. Between memory and hope we live, and we die trusting in the Triune God of relationship who says 'I remember' and 'I promise'.

8. Dermot Lane, *Keeping Hope Alive*, Dublin: Gill & Macmillan, 1996, p. 209.

Epilogue

All this was a long time ago, I remember,
And I would do it again, but set down
This set down
This: were we led all that way for
Birth or Death? There was a Birth, certainly,
We had evidence and no doubt. I had seen birth and death,
But had thought they were different; this Birth was
Hard and bitter agony for us, like Death, our death.
We returned to our places, these Kingdoms,
But no longer at ease here, in the old dispensation,
With an alien people clutching their gods.
I should be glad of another death.

T. S. Elliot, *Journey of the Magi*

Mystery and hope always come from the east. From there too came the wise men following a star. No doubt in their home place they celebrated strange rituals, indulged in astronomical calculations and read the ancient pagan religious texts of the eastern world. Anyone could see that these puzzling characters were up to something and nobody could see it more clearly than Herod the Great. Eastern folk might be smart when it comes to strange religions and astronomy but they know nothing about politics; Herod would deal with them when they returned.

They set off for Bethlehem with their gifts of gold, frankincense and myrrh; gold for a king, frankincense for a god and myrrh for a corpse. The one to whom they had come to do homage was kingly and divine yet destined for death. From the very beginning, Jesus' life had taken on a paschal character with this visit from the wise men of the east. As a result of a dream they returned to their country by another route. The other route from Bethlehem is always to Calvary. All of us would prefer to stick with the roads we know, given the security that comes from familiarity and the feeling that we are in control. But these strangers from the east are wise and they know that the false gods of familiarity, security and power have been thrown into question by the events in Bethlehem. Nothing would ever be the same again as the relationship between birth and death is posed anew.

The wise men did not stay in Bethlehem or Jerusalem to build a shrine or erect a monument. They returned to their kingdoms, not having embraced Judaism or Christianity but having learned a deeper lesson – they went home to die; to die to the false gods that can rule our lives and to embark on the final paschal journey that is death itself. All of us must follow the same journey as that of the Magi by dying to our cosy comfortable certainties through embracing the reality of Bethlehem and then moving onwards towards Calvary. For after Christ all rituals, all rites, all symbols are set in a new light; they must become paschal.

* * *

When you stand amongst the passage graves of Carrowkeel in Co Sligo, it is as if heaven and earth are joined together. For millennia people have come to this sacred place to honour the dead, to offer sacrifices to the gods and to celebrate the beauty and fertility of the earth at *Lughnasa* time. The footprints of the gods are everywhere to be seen; to the north the hills roll towards the sea while Ben Bulbin and Knocknarea rise defiantly in the distance; to the west the mysterious darkness of the Ox mountains folds onwards into Mayo; to the east the lake waters of Lough Arrow shimmer invitingly, whilst to the south the plains of Roscommon stretch as far as the eye can see. It is not surprising that our forebears came here to enact their rituals marking the thresholds of summer or winter, of a season or a year, of a new moon or a sunset, of birth or death. In these hills the mystery of life can be touched and evoked.

These rites of passage have characterised human civilisations since the mists of pre-history: from Carrowkeel to the country of the Magi and right down to today the significant passages in life are celebrated in ritual. To make these passages truly paschal is the task of Christian discipleship. But we have surely learned the sad lesson of history that the way to do this is not to break, burn and bury the remnants of earlier rituals and symbols, but rather to re-imagine what is given so that the form of Christ's pasch, already present in everything human, might be incarnated anew. For Christians, as the cover of this book suggests, the task is not to destroy but to let rituals speak of the divine power present in us and in our cosmos.

Standing amongst the passage graves of Carrowkeel the mystery of Christ's pasch is encountered in the beauty of this planet, the power of these ancient stones and the echo of distant rituals. Here there is *communitas* with the earth, with the dead and with all people who continue on the journey from passage to pasch.